Empty Your Mind

and

Achieve Your Dreams

Empty Your Mind

and

Achieve Your Dreams

Yogmata Keiko Aikawa

HIMALAYAN WISDOM SERIES

Natus Books
Barrytown, NY

Published by Natus Books
120 Station Hill Road
Barrytown, NY 12507

Natus Books is a publishing project of the Institute for Publishing Arts, a not-for-profit, tax-exempt organization [501(c)(3)].

Cover and interior design by Susan Quasha

ISBN: 978-1-58177-183-1

Library of Congress Control Number:2019942348

Manufactured in the United States of America

Contents

Introduction   3

1

Removing the Biases of the Mind: "Your Mind" Is Not Yourself

You Are Trying So Hard to Live, but Why?   7

Who, Exactly, Are You?   8

The Mind Seeks Objects of Dependence   9

The Constant Craving and Obsession of the Mind   10

Being Brainwashed by Society   11

The Mind Moves in the Space Between Positive and Negative   12

Positive Thinking Is One-Sided   13

Awareness of Yourself   15

There are Stages to Awareness   16

The Meaning of Achieving Harmony   17

Being Aware, Yourself, of What Is Going on Now   18

By Being Thought-Free, You and Your Surroundings Come Alive   19

2

You Can Be Happy if You Can Discard Things You Value

Becoming Suffocated by Taking on Burdens   21

Attachment to "Appearance"   21

The Courage to Boldly Release Important Things   22

Bring in Life Energy by Breathing, Ridding the Mind of Toxins   24

Breathing Method to Enhance Life Energy and
    Attain a Tranquil Mind   24
The Trick to Happiness Is Release   25
Creatively Starting Again   26
Change Is an Opportunity for Thanks   28
Difficult Times Are Also Chances for Learning   29
Gratitude for Being in Difficult Circumstances   30
Having Love and Cleansing Negative Thoughts   31

3

**All Outcomes Are Created by Your Mind: If You
DesireSomething, It Can Be Realized**

Don't Be Bound by Meaningless Rules   33
The Trick to Making Living Easy   34
Know That "My Mind Is Not Me"   35
Why You Make the Same Mistakes Over and Over   36
The Mind Draws Unhappiness and Disaster as Well   37
The Mind's Habit of Blaming Other People   38
Change the Mind and Its Surroundings Will Also
    Change   39
Think That the Head Does Not Exist   40
Empty Your Mind, Let Go of the Ego   41
If You Ask for It, It Can Be Granted   42
There Is Wisdom, Power, and Love   43
Yagya and Diksha, Meditation That Grants Wishes   44

4

The Path I Walked: Training in the Himalayas, and Achievement of Samadhi

The Grace of the Himalayas	45
Memories of Childhood	46
The Walking Race When I Was in Junior High School	47
The Words I Said to My Mother One Day	48
My Encounter with Yoga	49
When I Looked Deep into my Mind	50
Pursue True Peace of Mind	51
The Himalayan Guru Pilot Babaji	52
The Journey to the Himalayas: The Place from the Ramayana	53
Beautiful Scenery and Plain Faith	54
Training on Pindari Glacier	55
Becoming One's True Self in Samadhi	56
Enlightenment: An Experience Beyond Death	57
Samadhi Through Practice and Sankalpa	58
Searching for the True Master	59
Hari Babaji and Ottar Babaji	59
Meeting the Great Sage Hari Babaji	60
Testimonial: She Performed Many Miracles	61
Diksha Awakens the Inner Self and Changes That Person's Fate	62
The Grace Anugraha	63
From Practicing for Oneself to Practicing for Others	64
Demonstrate and Communicate Truth	65
To Holy Kailas with Pilot Babaji	66
Things That Remind Me of the Himalayas	67

5

The Teachings of the Himalayas: True Yoga

Balance Is a Part of What Yoga Means   70

The Teachings of Yoga and Harmony of Mind and
Body   71

The First Step of Yoga: Yama   72

Purification: The Second Step, Niyama   73

The Meaning Behind Asceticism and Reciting
Mantras   74

Testimonial: The Nation's Top Year-on-Year Sales   75

The Third Step of Yoga: Asana   76

To Be Able to Naturally Solve Many Problems   77

The Meaning of the Tree Pose   78

Asana Is Moving Meditation   80

Order the Breath, Cleanse the Body and Mind: Step
Four, Pranayama   80

A Mind That Sees Without Getting Trapped: Step
Five, Pratyahara   81

Cleansing of the Senses and Cleansing of the Mind   83

Gaining True Freedom by Cleansing the Senses   84

Becoming One with the Holy Energy   85

Gain Power Through Spiritual Unity: Step Six,
Dharana   86

Step Seven, Meditation and Dhyana; and Step Eight,
Samadhi   87

To Become the True Self   88

Unpublicized Himalayan Yoga   89

Your Body Is Changeable   89

6

From Religion to That Which Transcends Religion:
Himalayan Masters, Gautama Siddhartha, and Jesus Christ

The Mind's Anchor in Painful Times   91

"You Have To" Obsessions in Spiritual Teachings   92

What Buddha (Sakyamuni) Investigated   93

Meditation to Samadhi—Christ's Case   94

What Religious Faith Brings About   95

Teachings of the Himalayan Sages in Oral Tradition   97

Meeting the Right Master Is Important   98

Returning to the True Self Is the Truth Indeed   98

The Existence That Guides from Darkness to Light   100

Basics of Safe Practice and Yoga   101

The Most Important Waves of the Source   102

Be Purified by Sacred Waves   103

Sending Sacred Waves to You   104

Lessons of the Paths of Faith and Love   105

Testimonial: Receiving Diksha as a Family   106

Thoughts Fly like Arrows   107

The Path of Energy   108

Techniques for Changing   109

The Amazing Power Within   111

When Chakras Are Activated   111

7

What Is God? What Is Karma? God's Existence and Us

God Is Embodied in Many Energies   113

After the Outer Pilgrimage Is Over   114

You Are God's Shrine   115

What Is Karma?   116

The Truth About Reincarnation   117

Karma Appears and Disappears Without Fail   117

Karma from Past Lives   118

When Ingrained Karmic Memories Manifest as
    Phenomena   119

*Testimonial: Making Others Happy Through
    Meditation*   120

Karma Is Also Recorded in the Universe   121

How to Purify Karma   122

Meditation Methods for Purifying Karma Quickly   123

Knowing the Appropriate Use of the Physical Body   124

Testimonial: Samadhi Meditation Guides Me   125

Preparation from the Original Energy   127

8

Mind, Body, and Soul: The Painful Thoughts of Those Who Choose Suicide

Even After Suicide, the Soul Doesn't Die   130

When Someone Takes Their Life, The Soul Suffers   131

Put All Your Effort into Doing What You've Been
    Given to Do Now   131

The Relationship between Mind, Body, and Soul   133

The Mind's Memory Remains in the Spirit   134

Do So-Called Heaven and Paradise Exist?   135

Heaven and Hell Are Right There Beside You   135

Our Existence Comes from the Source   136

Light and Sound in the Universe   137

Praising Pure Consciousness   138

9

Returning to the True Self through Meditation: The Process of Transformation

The Importance of Meditation in Life   140

Maha Yoga Breathing Meditation Method   141

Training for Absence of Thought   141

Breathe Idle Thoughts into the Void   142

Experiencing Absence of Thought   143

The Process of Change Through Meditation   144

Testimonial: Meditation Has Made Childrearing
  Easy and Fun   144

Inner Peace Meditation   145

No More Needless Fear and Detours   146

Drop Habits and Return the Mind and Body to
  Their Natural State   147

Meditation Is Also Practice to Skillfully Transcend
  Death   148

Know That Everything Has an Outside and an
  Inside   148

A Method to Clear Away Wrongdoing and Dirt   149

Meditate Daily, a Little at a Time, with the Feeling
  of Brushing Your Teeth   151

Testimonial: Thinking Disappears, the Body
  Disappears, and Meditation Occurs   152

Doing Meditation Your Own Way Is Dangerous   152

The Soul Will Fly Where You Want to Go   153

Testimonial: One-and-a-Half Years Since
  Beginning Meditation   154

Only Those Who Experience Samadhi Can Show
  the True Path   155

10

Truths About the Soul and the World After Death

The Words of Mediums and Channelers 157

It's Dangerous if Your Mind Power Becomes Strong 158

It's Essential to Purify the Mind Before
    Strengthening Mind Power 159

The Truth About Seeing Past Lives 160

A Guide Is Needed for Progress on the Spiritual
    Path 161

Testimonial: I Became Able to Reject Bad Energy 162

What Happens When People Die? 163

A Story of Rebirth 164

What Is Your Guardian Angel? 165

The Holy Existence Called Angels 166

Auras Are the Light of Energy 167

Cases of Spirit Possession 167

When Channelers Contact Spirits 168

*Testimonial: People Tell Me I've Become a
    Different Person* 169

Don't Stop at Being Self-Satisfied with
    Volunteering 170

By Turning Awareness Inward, Become a Person
    Who Doesn't Blame Others 171

Ignorance Hurts People Unknowingly 172

11

Prayer Opens the Door to the Future: Seeking the Origin of Human Beings

Why Is There Divinity in Humans?   174

The Occasions That Awaken the Divinity Within
    Ourselves   175

Know That All Things Are God's Creation   176

The Relationship Between Modern Medicine and
    Spiritual Healing   177

A Mind of Belief Brings Success and Health   178

Healings Brought by the Body's Energy   178

Expelling Toxins by Purifying the Five Senses   180

Yantras and Mantras that Purify the Mind and
    Heal Sickness   181

Prayer Directed to the Heart   182

The Tremendous Power Called Prayer   183

Afterword   185

About the Author   188

Connect with Himalayan Wisdom   189

Empty Your Mind

and

Achieve Your Dreams

Introduction

Release from Worry

We all have worries. We worry about our families, our futures, our pasts. Even if we are going about our daily lives quite happily, our minds tend to stop working smoothly when a problem arises. Problems are things we want to escape; we don't enjoy the uncertainties and difficulties they create.

Our minds are powerful and can create a multitude of things. In the course of our lives, various desires manifest, and, because of the information overload of modern society, rubbish and debris build up in our minds, creating confusion. However, we tend not to realize that our minds are so cluttered, just as we tend not to notice our state of mind or way of behaving at any given time. We live our lives unaware, and our behavior becomes our destiny.

However, when we experience pain, we become aware of the mind's existence, and the disordered nature of our thoughts. Such times can, in fact, be regarded as opportunities that allow us to examine our way of living. What is the purpose, exactly, of our existence? The question itself is an opportunity. We are being shown a path—the path to our personal growth.

Receiving Instruction from the Great Yoga Masters

The universe is as beautiful as it is limitless. The stars, moon, and sun are constantly in motion. Here on earth we have mountains, rivers, oceans, flowing clouds, and growing vegetation—all of nature, shining beautifully. Each and every one of us is nurtured in this great universe. But, although we were born into the grace of our parents'

3

love and the love of the universe, we seem to wander aimlessly, and easily become confused or depressed.

If you read this book, your confused mind will change; it will become bright, calm, and filled with joy. I have researched and practiced Yoga since fatefully coming into contact with it when I was in high school. At that time, I was grappling with such questions as "What is the mind?" and "Why do we live?" and, while teaching Yoga, I pursued further questions of body, mind, and spirit. Not satisfied with the answers I was able to find, I sought deeper truths and continued my training in various parts of India. In the Himalayas, where God is said to live, I underwent many years of rigorous training known as samadhi training, the path to God.

Then, finally, through a connection with the holy man Pilot Babaji, I was able to meet the Yoga Mahatma Hari Babaji in the Himalayan interior. This was a very rare and decidedly fortunate occurrence. When I first met him and he spoke to me, I was so moved I couldn't stop my tears from welling up.

From that training and from my own personal training after that, I applied what I had learned to my daily life. My efforts were recognized, and I received the grace of God known as Anugraha from Mahatma Hari Babaji. Eventually I became the first woman and foreigner, not only in India but in the world, to become a Himalayan Siddha master (that is, a complete master); I received the title Yogmata ("Mother of Yoga") and the spiritual name Keladevi Giri. Additionally, I was conferred with the title Maha Mahamandaleshwar ("The Great Master of the Universe"), the highest instructor title of Juna Akhara (the spiritual society of India).

With the full approval of the government of India, I became the first woman in history to perform a public samadhi, the biggest meditation event associated with Yoga philosophy. During a public samadhi—which I have

4

now performed eighteen times—I attain a state of oneness with the Godhead and realize the Brahman-Atman identity; the earth is cleansed, and people's minds are purified. While demonstrating through this experience the existence of what is written in the holy books as "the path transcending life and death" and "an enlightened state of mind," I have bestowed blessings on over a hundred thousand people who have visited public samadhis, not only from India, but from all over the world.

The Teachings of the Himalayas

The teachings of the Himalayas have been continuously transmitted for over five thousand years; they constitute an unchanging truth. This book is a transmission of these teachings, written in plain, easy-to-understand language, for those who live in today's world.

By reading this book, you will come to understand the true nature of the suffering and uncertainty you have experienced thus far. You will also come to understand the reasons why you experienced this pain. You will be able to pump the truth from the deep well within; this will make it easier for you to live, and will bring you freedom. You will come to know a new way of living, and you will be able to make it a part of you.

You will realize that our true nature is wonderfully rich and that our existence is rich with abundance and possibility. Our everyday encounters, each and every casual moment—all are luminous, overflowing with tenderness and beauty. Furthermore, you will come to notice that your thoughts and behavior are directly connected to the world at large.

Even though you will be frequenting the same places and spending time with the same people as before, something will strike you as different: the world will have transformed and become deeply beautiful, and everything you encounter will be bathed in the light of gentle love. Your life will feel far more complete, and you will soon notice that it has completely changed.

The secret teachings of the Himalayas overflow with majestic love and the grace of God known as Anugraha. They will bring you true happiness and, furthermore, lead you to enlightenment.

YOGMATA KEIKO AIKAWA

I

Removing the Biases of the Mind: "Your Mind" Is Not Yourself

You Are Trying So Hard to Live, But Why?

There are people who are desperately attempting to realize their desires: "I want to be more beautiful," "I want to increase my abilities," "I want my family to get along," "I want peace of mind," "I want to be well again," etc. There are also people who are consumed by worry and doubt: "Why do I feel so anxious, even though I'm trying so hard?" "Each day is so dull; I just want *something* to happen."

I have lost count of how many people have come to me seeking solutions to such problems. What can be done to enable a life without worry and pain, a more abundant life of hope and fulfillment? To answer this, we must understand what real happiness is.

We spend our lives in the physical bodies and minds we have been given. However, most of us remain unaware of what abundant living—truly joyful living—really is. Because of this, we tire ourselves out in pursuit of a transient, counterfeit happiness. If we were able to know our true selves, we would be able to rid ourselves of worry and suffering. My aim is for you to find the way to your true self through reading this book.

What, then, should you do in order to know your true self? The first step is to love yourself deeply. If you can do that, your "inside" will become filled with joy and gratitude, and your mind will become peaceful. You will be able to believe in yourself because you feel at ease. This may seem abstract and hard to understand, but I will explain, step by step, what has to be done.

I speak about the meaning of life to those who consult me in person. Here are some of their words: "My life has become easier, thanks to you. I feel as if a burden I carried for a long time has been lifted from me." "I assumed until now that I was a person with bad luck, and I hated every day. But after listening to you talk, my gloomy outlook greatly improved." If you are able to love yourself, you are also able to love those around you. If you do that, you will not only feel at ease with yourself, but those around you will also feel at ease and become happy. A woman who was continuously at odds with her boss at work and who furiously exclaimed to me, "There's no way I can forgive such a tyrannical person!" eventually told me, with relief, "I've understood that my boss is also in a tough, stressful position." If everyone could feel at ease, there would be more happiness and peace in the world.

Who, Exactly, Are You?

I would like to ask those of you who are reading this book for the first time the following four questions:

"Where does your bitterness come from?"

"Where did your body and mind come from?"

"What is inside you?"

"Who, exactly, are you?"

You might respond to these questions with, "I am myself," or, "I am me." But is this really the case? In order to know your true self, it is necessary to doubt the truth of such assertions. You were born the child of your parents, you have a name that is your own, you likely graduated from such-and-such a school before starting work, etc.— these are facts that cannot be denied. However, is the you that has a job and a physical body and the ability to think really the real you?

We casually use such expressions as "I think this" or "I am sick." But when you say "I think," is it what the *real* you thinks? Isn't it actually the case that it's not "you" that thinks, but "your mind?" Are "you" and "your mind" the same thing? And when you say "I am sick," isn't it "your body" or "your mind" that actually has the illness? Your body and mind are not you yourself. They are in reality only "outward expressions." Let me repeat: the afflicted mind is not you yourself. Your body is also not you. What is afflicted is not you, but your body and mind.

Try to think about things this way: when you waver, the real you, which looks at the wavering mind with a detached gaze, is actually in a different place. If you can think like this, your affliction and doubt will be greatly reduced. That which gives power to the mind and body, the life-giving existence, is your true self. This is purity and freedom, the original existence that empowers all things.

The Mind Seeks Objects of Dependence

What, then, is the mind? The first thing I would like you to know is that the mind is a type of energy and is the controller of the body. It follows that the mind has direction, characteristic strengths, and various proclivities. One of these proclivities is what is called "always seeking objects of dependence." The first obstacle we encounter when we begin to explore our minds is this "dependence." And here, in fact, is where we can find answers to the questions of why the mind tends to lean toward the negative, and why we are always swayed by this kind of mind.

People sometimes externalize worry, sadness, and pain, which ends up going nowhere. Because nothing comes of this, they try to forget about their distress and, on the verge of loneliness, they come to depend on external things. This is because such dependence makes our lives easier on the surface. In the modern era, there are many convenient things we can enjoy and subsequently depend on. We watch television, talk with friends, go shopping, take trips, go out to concerts or the theater, etc. We believe that, in this way, if we possess many things, acquire knowledge, and live a comfortable life, we are sure to enrich our hearts. The mind's desire responds immediately to the things we see, hear, and taste—stimulation that enters through the senses; it works to obtain such things, and usually succeeds.

Having said this, though, are we really able to be satisfied by such things? No. Far from it. It is the nature of human beings to crave, to have an increased desire for the next thing, to want more. It is true that the senses and mind are temporarily satisfied, but before long the next desire arises, and the mind seeks further satisfaction. In this way, we continually embrace the idea of want and become obsessed with things, money, people, and that which lies outside of ourselves.

The Constant Craving and Obsession of the Mind

In today's world, there are those who live lives of wealth, and those who do not—the haves and the have nots. We are all different, but many of us are attached to the idea that we are unfulfilled deep inside, that something is missing. Although this may be true for those who have not been able to acquire external things, it is equally true for those who *have* been able to do so.

This is because everything that people have obtained or owned is due to sensation and the satisfaction of the mind. Desires are longings for things that the mind needs, and, as we will discuss further on, are born from what is called a person's *karma*—the memory of the experience of all past actions.

Karma always keeps our minds busy. Being satisfied with having obtained one thing, we immediately want the next, and our desire gradually escalates. Then, if we can't obtain what we desire, we not only become restless and depressed, but we compare ourselves with those who have obtained what we desire, and we become jealous and envious as a result.

Our minds constantly want something—some kind of movement. They are busy in pursuit of knowledge, beauty, material wealth, satisfaction of the ego, and satisfaction of others' expectations. Such minds have created many convenient things, made advances in the arts, and helped to develop our cultures. However, capable as our minds are, they eventually lose interest without having experienced satisfaction. This results in a gradual separation from our true selves, an obsession with external things, and an endless expansion of our desires. In this way, we lose our peace of mind. No matter how many times this is repeated, the game never ends.

In order to avoid this, we have to look at ourselves deeply and develop control of the mind. *All uncertainty and dissatisfaction are born of the mind's desire for external things.* We have to look closely at ourselves and ask what is true. Is life really about keeping the mind busy in the pursuit of external things? We have to look closely at if life is really about keeping our mind busy, if life is really about obtaining external things.

Being Brainwashed by Society

In our quest for happiness and our desire for a rich life, we meet many people and come to own many things. We read books that are said to be beneficial, go to hear lectures and talks by those who are active in society, and learn from our parents, teachers, and mentors.

Nevertheless, most of us don't know what real happiness is. We try to be happy in the present by imitating those around us and listening to what our superiors tell us. We are, in other words, brainwashed by society. We feel secure when we are doing the same as those around us; it is little surprise, then, that most of us behave in the same way. The term "following blindly" describes this pattern of behavior. If something becomes fashionable, we feel that we need to buy it, and, in no time at all, we own it. Then, after using it for a few days, we grow tired of it, and soon can hardly bear to look at it.

In this way, we become captivated not by eternal things, but by that which we soon grow tired of, living each day in confusion, as if nibbling on things and then throwing them away, always nibbling and throwing away. We are swayed by the influence of everything around us, no longer able to look at ourselves clearly. What, then, should we do?

There is no getting around the taste of satisfaction from external things, which is enjoyable to the senses and to the mind. What is important is to ask yourself, "Who am I?" and "Are the mind and feelings that experience joy and hardship really my true self?" and, after contemplating these questions, to arrive at knowledge of your true self. To put it another way, you need to be able to control your mind through being aware of it, rather than be controlled by your mind.

The Mind Moves in the Space Between Positive and Negative

Depression is a big problem in our society. Depression happens: 1) when you generate excessive stress by fixating and obsessing about oneself or others, or through overuse of the negative mind; 2) when you use too much energy by living in constant uncertainty; and 3) when you use excessive energy and lose balance through overly strong thoughts.

We are all capable of becoming depressed. Our minds don't constantly think positive thoughts; rather, they move back and forth between positive and negative. Modern medicine is having difficulty in addressing this. While the mind is a wonderful and mysterious thing, if it becomes slightly unbalanced, it changes completely and becomes troublesome indeed. People's minds are strange; in order to satisfy, we first notice our deficiency and then try to satiate it. When this happens, we just see the deficiencies in ourselves and cannot notice our good points or that we are already fulfilled. Most people unconsciously search only for that which is lacking, exacerbating the feelings of discontent, which causes distress.

We then become convinced that this is the norm, not realizing that it is precisely our actions that are causing us this pain.

But, again, let me repeat: if we are able to take a close look at how we are fulfilled, we will find it possible to escape from negativity.

Positive Thinking Is One-Sided

Positive thinking is one of the first things that comes to mind as a method of escape from depression and distress. It is important to try to be positive in any situation. However, if you make a mistake, simply shifting into positive thinking is escapism and self-protection for the sake of convenience. This is understandable at times, of course, because, out of negative perfectionism, we blame things on ourselves and others, thereby creating additional pain for ourselves. Wouldn't it be better if our experiences somehow acted as a stimulus for our personal growth?

Positive thinking by itself may cause us to disregard useful opportunities for closely examining ourselves; if we don't take time to reflect, our egos have a tendency to swell. Try to closely examine yourself and your surrounding circumstances. Are you always angry? Does your heart feel distressed? Are you always worrying? Do you have trouble sleeping? Do you notice your own anger tortures your heart, too much worry causes insomnia and makes you sick. Try to move beyond such circumstances; try to become a person who makes positive choices. Depending on the circumstances, it may be a good thing to be blissfully positive, even if this concerns the workings of the mind only. But it is so much better to become a person who is attentive and able to understand how things are constructed. And you can best become such a person by accepting yourself as you are.

Numerous things can make us depressed: we can't find a reason for living; we don't know what to do with our lives; we become fixated on some small thing that we continue to fail to understand; or we have unrealistic expectations or fantasies that our families and friends simply don't understand.

The need to establish ourselves, live happily and creatively, and experience self-fulfillment can in itself become a big source of pressure. Perfectionists can become arrogant and impatient, which in turn creates suffering. Rather than growing, as we aim to do, our physical strength and energy become depleted, we spiral into self-loathing, and become lethargic and depressed.

I urge you to love yourself as you are, regardless of whether you can or can't do something or if something isn't working for you. There is no particular or pressing need to become a special person. The important thing is to be here, now. Household cleaning and mundane daily tasks are perfectly important. If you are able to do the things that are given to you, the things you must do, without any special thought, a path will be opened for you.

Acceptance and awareness are crucial. In addition, the grace of esoteric Himalayan Anugraha will release stress and obsessions from the mind, allowing you to overflow with essential confidence, returning you to a state of peace. Your mind will become free, you will become accepting of reality, and you will once more be able to live with ease.

Awareness of Yourself

In order to know yourself, you need to be aware of your state of mind at any given moment. This is easy to say, but by no means easy to do. For example, let's say that a normally reserved person lets their guard down after drinking too much alcohol, and complains to someone they don't know. Such things happen because we are unable to be aware of ourselves and our condition when drunk. The brake of the intellect, which is usually applied, is no longer effective. It takes practice, then, to maintain an awakened awareness so that we can notice what happens around us in the present moment. Not being aware isn't really so different from being drunk.

It may seem obvious to say, but our eyes and ears face outward, thereby improving our ability to catch hold of external things. For this reason, we desperately try not to miss anything from the outside, but, at the same time, we ignore our inside—we don't listen to our own inner voice. However, by using the secret methods and teachings of the Himalayan Siddha masters, you can objectively observe the self and its grumbles and complaints—loneliness, anger, and the like—and at the same time feel relief. You will gradually be able to approach the things that you keep in the depths of your heart and be able to view external things with love.

If you peel off the layers of the self—in much the same way as you peel the layers of skin off an onion—you will eventually come to understand the "voice of the truth and the true form" that is at your core. If, by doing this, you can understand the way you should truly live, true abundance will expand inside you, giving birth to the feeling that you are actually, and truly, alive. This is awareness, coming to know truth.

There are Stages to Awareness

By viewing things from the perspective of truth, you can gradually throw away those things you don't need and live more simply. You can observe without being caught up in things, and only use what is necessary, rather than swallowing everything whole. This is what we mean by *awareness*. Awareness evolves through progress in meditative training: Siddha masters possess high-dimensional energy, which can protect you while you gradually realize awareness. Then, if you arrive at the truth through awareness, it becomes connected to the attainment of your true self, and eventually you will come to be able to see God.

There are stages to awareness; I will explain them simply. First, you must observe the body. By observing your body without being caught up by what is inside and what is outside, you should be able to understand it. Eventually, a feeling of gratitude will be born that transcends the usual likes and dislikes. Next, observe the senses. By observing the five senses, you should be able to restore their correct functions and become balanced. Then, observe the emotions. You will become able to see many emotions, such as crankiness, impatience, jealousy, anger, and sadness. By ridding yourself of your attachment to such emotions, you will be able to transcend them.

The next step is to observe the mind, in all its aspects. You will encounter thinking, analyzing, and judging, among others, as well as the mind of the present and the mind of the past. By doing this, you will come to be able to see what is called "past lives," the mind that has been deeply etched into you by prior existence. You must also observe your breath and your energy. By progressing through these stages of meditation training step by step, you will finally be able to achieve true awareness. In other words, awakening. Enlightenment.

The Meaning of Achieving Harmony

If you live with awareness, and are practicing meditation for awareness, you are always able to return to your center, and your surrounding circumstances will not cause you to waver. If you are not anchored in your center, you will encounter things that trouble you, even though you may at times feel quite encouraged.

This is because constantly doing the same thing is a mental as well as a physical habit. If you become fixated on something, even something good, you will end up using your mind and body in a lopsided manner and will never achieve harmony. You must therefore undertake to achieve harmony by deepening awareness and releasing attachments.

The harmony I speak of here is Yoga, which means to tie together. If everything is tied together with love, harmony, and gratitude, it becomes one; purity is achieved, and your true self appears. This is the heart of the esoteric Himalayan teachings. Everything in the universe is constituted by this natural law, this one deep truth. It can be awakened by the power of Anugraha.

Because of the overemphasis on desire in modern life, there is a tendency to go running off in all directions, not through limitless love, but according to judgmental mind, which is forever sorting things into piles of likes and dislikes. Because of this, the harmony and balance of the mind and body is eventually broken. This is the same in personal relationships. Once a person or thing catches our attention, energy immediately flows in that direction, as if a switch has been flipped. As a result, our disposition becomes "Like! Like! Like!" Attachment increases, and we become unable to detach ourselves.

On the other hand, we tend to completely block things that we don't like, saying, "No! No! No!" However, even though we don't like these things and make an effort to distance ourselves, they sap our energy as negative attachments as long as we remain fixated on avoiding them.

The general method followed in order to change something is to do something about it; let me here describe the more profound method set forth in the secret Himalayan teachings. You must first learn to stop the activity of the mind, and observe, simply as you are. This is done without like or dislike, without flipping the mind's switch on or off. Return to the pure mind of "simply being there." This is what I would like you to practice. This is the release from attachment and a return to a state of balance in all areas of experience. It is also the ultimate path.

The mind is strong, so it will obstruct your attempts to simply observe. Accept these attempts and observe them as well. The love and strength of the esoteric Himalayan teachings will prevent distractions and support your simple observance without action. Through receiving the grace of the Himalayan teachings, it is possible to purify the mind of its habits and attachments, and to become free. In this situation, awareness naturally emerges without any training.

Being Aware, Yourself, of What Is Going on Now

Because modern society is so distracting, there is a strong tendency for our minds to be directed outward, leaving no opportunity for inward reflection. However, if we are able to look inside ourselves, new thoughts and fresh ideas will likely rise to the surface. Normally, our minds are occupied by something and become synchronized with it, and so it prevents us to see inside of ourselves. It is important to practice directly suspending the mind and looking inward without taking any action. If you can do this, you will be able to see your internal state more clearly, and, further, the state of external things, and to deepen your understanding of these things.

Eventually, you will notice that you were attached to unnecessary things that surfaced inside, which you then misinterpreted as important, perhaps extremely important. You will come to see many things, such as how you have been living, what your attitudes and nature have been, how people around you have behaved, and so on. This work is at times painful and at times enjoyable, but it will certainly deepen your perception and establish a base on which to construct a more abundant self.

Because most people are so caught up in their own thoughts, they are unable to open their ears to the opinions of others. It happens that, when we separate our minds from being caught up like this, we are able to think, "Ah, there are different ways of thinking about things!"

By Being Thought-Free, You and Your Surroundings Come Alive

If we deepen our awareness of what's inside us, the mind of worry and hostility disappears, leaving a mind of peaceful stillness in its place. When this happens, other people will gravitate toward you.

Imagine this scenario: you are on a trip in Africa, when suddenly a lion comes running toward you. With a split second in which to decide, how do you respond? Sensing danger approaching, do you quickly run and find a safe place to hide? Or do you take up a weapon and run at the lion yourself? Those stricken by fear and those who rise up to face the lion both experience a sudden discharge of the hormone adrenaline, a stimulant that is part of the body's system. This provides the energy to confront the lion. If you were to project this energy, there's no doubt that the lion would sense it and attack you. The lion is programmed by its self-defense instinct to bite moving things. As we can understand by watching pet cats, they practice hunting prey from the time they are young. If it were to come to a battle of power or speed, you would never win.

What then, should you do? This may sound surprising, and what I am suggesting is by no means easy, but, if you were able to project an energy of love and peace that said, "You and I are brothers," you might have a chance of surviving. If, for example, you had been raised from childhood to have no fear of lions, you would be able to face the lion with a natural disposition, and it would be possible to win the lion over. That is, if you didn't project fear or aggression, and faced the lion with an attitude of naturalness, it's possible the lion wouldn't attack you.

This principle holds whether the other party is a lion or a human being. If you become convinced that the person in front of you has an offensive nature, you will find it difficult not to respond to them in an adversarial way. If this happens, the other person will sense your negative energy and respond in kind. How much better it would be to stand before this person completely unprotected, in a state of innocence or no-mind. No adversarial energies would result. If we progress further from the state of no-mind and become our true selves, the mind's uncertainty and adversarial spirit disappear, resulting in a pure, harmonious existence. Once this happens, the energy emitted is immediately attractive to others.

The fundamental truths regarding what is right and what is wrong, and how to determine the pros and cons of a particular action, are simple. It is not your ego that is important; rather, it is the vivid life of your true self and the vivid life of the other person, and the relationship between the two. A moderate state of balance is the first step toward allowing trust and love to be born.

If you can awaken your awareness and free your mind from its usual captive state, you will come to understand what is good and right.

2

You Can Be Happy if You Can Discard Things You Value

Becoming Suffocated by Taking on Burdens

We have a strong sense that our happiness will increase in tandem with the number of things we own. Because of this, we expend great effort in the pursuit of titles, money, and knowledge. The value of these things changes over time. Our jobs and titles must be relinquished upon retirement, and money is meaningless unless it is spent. But, because life is uncertain and we worry about the future, we constantly collect things, thinking that, the more we have, the better off we are. But, all too quickly, our attachments become ties that bind us—isn't this the state of most people today?

We fight to get a good job, to get a high position, to receive love and trust from family and friends, for health, for good grades, and even when we attain these and have success and happiness within our grasp, the struggle continues because our expectations only increase. Eventually, we start to feel crushed under their weight; at times, we feel as though we might suffocate. It is vital, then, that we become aware of the things that are truly important to us. Being aware of these things will help us to answer the question of how we should live our lives.

Attachment to "Appearance"

"When I got old, everybody suddenly stopped being my friend." The person who voiced this complaint to me was a woman in her thirties. Now, I am clearly in trouble if someone in their thirties thinks they are old, but it seems that lots of people feel this way. In Japanese society today there is a strong tendency to make a fuss about young women, and the women themselves tend to think, "If I'm over thirty, I'm over the hill." If you think like this, you will certainly create a difficult situation for yourself.

The important thing is your frame of mind. If you can change your mind to think, "Age doesn't matter. It's not how I'm viewed from the outside, but my inner beauty that's important," your confidence will increase and new friends who hold similar values will appear. You must try to let go of your assumptions. If you can do this, you will become attractive in a way that has nothing to do with age. Through deepening your awareness, becoming pure, and approaching your true essence, you will be able to love yourself, and your life will be enriched.

The Courage to Boldly Release Important Things

Most of us feel some attachment to beautiful things. Beauty is certainly a wonderful thing, but most of our attachments concern external things, which can change, and are never constant. I am not suggesting you abandon any interest in beautiful things, but I want you to go further, and to express your own natural, harmonious beauty.

Much of history can be described in terms of mankind's repeated and desperate attempts to plunder—that is, to obtain by force—that which it desires. We earnestly hold on to such things, even the things we don't need, and are reluctant to give them to others. And not just the physical objects we see with our eyes—we jealously hoard our knowledge and experience as well. Do our hearts grow, become more abundant and expansive, as a result? No. On the contrary, we merely become further enslaved by our ignorance, desire, and confusion.

If we can learn to be aware of what is going on inside ourselves, we will likely discover that our knowledge and aspirations are accompanied by obsession and pretension, our passions and sympathies accompanied by feelings of envy and dissatisfaction.

In order to live a life of true value, it is necessary to accept that these things are there and practice not being captivated by them, and to have the courage to boldly let go of anything and everything. In this process, your heavy heart will become light, and your mind will become truly eased. Throw away the negative mind, and, along with it, the rubbish of pretension, obsession, and superiority. In the final stage (of reaching true self) you must throw away even joy itself; otherwise, your mind will still shroud the truth, and you will not be able to become the far more abundant true self that lies beyond such worldly joy.

Often, even if we are determined to throw everything away, when we come to actually do it, we find that we can't. Throwing things away is difficult, especially when it comes to such relatively intangible things as knowledge and desire. Most of us want to look good and to enjoy a decent standard of living—all of this, too, must be thrown away. By throwing away those parts of the mind that are consumed by "I choose that over this," we can purify successive layers of the multifaceted mind, and eventually empty it. Let me be clear about this phrase, "throwing away": as you become your true self, these superficial things will naturally separate and fall away. Then you will truly be given harmony and love and come to become the creative existence at the origin of all things. We experience pain because we cling to the mind and the fabrications it creates. How much easier our lives would be if we would only clear all of this away!

Bring in Life Energy by Breathing, Ridding the Mind of Toxins

Let me introduce you to one method of throwing out the rubbish of the mind. It is possible, through awareness, to cleanse the mind of its toxins (desires). The secret teachings of the esoteric Himalayan wisdom contain different methods of purification, but one of the easiest and most effective is breathing, which is a wonderful tool that can effectively cleanse the mind.

The following breathing method is easy and safe and, if performed wholeheartedly, has a tremendously cleansing effect. Through it, your energy will be cleansed, and you will become balanced and able to control your mind. When you breathe in, you are taking in life energy; when you breathe out, you are expelling toxins. Be careful not to concentrate *only* on breathing out; balance is crucial. Try to place equal importance on breathing in *and* breathing out.

Breathing Method to Enhance Life Energy and Attain a Tranquil Mind

Sit on the floor with both legs extended. Bend the lower half of your left leg inward. Next, bend in the lower half of your right leg. Extend your spinal column. If you have stiff hip joints, you may find it helpful to place a cushion under your buttocks. If you find this position unstable, you may prefer to use a chair. Just be sure to extend your spinal column.

Expel breath from your mouth with the intention of releasing toxins. Abandon the toxins of the body. Abandon the rubbish and grime that has accumulated in the mind. Expel all of the air in your lungs and draw your stomach in.

Next, breathe in slowly and deeply, through your nose. Breathe in the *prana*—the life energy of the universe.

Repeat this thirty times, then breathe naturally. Be intently aware of the flow of your breath, in and out. Continue this for about five minutes.

Often, people who are ill either exhale too strongly, or can only inhale with ease and have difficulty exhaling. In other words, they aren't balanced. Exhalation, called *apana*, is associated with death; its energy carries things to the outside, cleaning the inside. Inhalation, *prana*, is the energy that supports life. These two energies have a center that is constantly in balance, which is called *chuyo*, the middle path. This is harmony—Yoga.

The human body has seven energy centers called *chakras*. These exist in the tailbone, sacrum, abdomen, chest, throat, middle of the forehead, and at the crown of the head. The seven chakras coincide with the body's nerve plexuses and hormone centers. If there is insufficient prana in these centers, weakness and compromised movement can ensue. By first adjusting the breathing and cleansing the chakras, you can cleanse your energy even further and cause your energy centers to awaken.

The breath shows the condition of the mind, and life energy is generated by one's self (one's true self) and supplied to the mind. The mind, then, can be controlled through this energy.

The Trick to Happiness Is Release

If the body becomes weak and we are unable to exhale what we have inhaled, our life may be put at risk. If we only eat and are unable to excrete, we become constipated, which can cause illness. If we buy new things and don't throw anything away, our house will soon overflow. Regardless of context, the natural flow is such that, when we bring something in, we send something out. Keeping something in hand without throwing something away shows confusion within oneself.

We certainly feel pain when we lose something. We find it difficult to endure the loss of money or possessions, and especially the loss of our health, regardless of our intention. However, it might be useful to think about things in another way. Losing our wallet, for example, is beneficial to the person who finds it. The mind can quickly be changed in this way. If we can approach experience in this way, we will be able to part from unnecessary attachments and know peace of mind.

It is difficult, of course, to approach our misfortunes in this way, but you must try to exude positive energy while increasing your awareness, without judging the actions of those around you, and without becoming captivated by external things. In other words, you must practice giving. You must practice giving love.

Even in our closest friendships, a greedy heart will soon cause distrust, and a quarrel or disagreement may result. If, on the other hand, we open our hearts wide, expecting nothing in return, simply giving love, gratitude, and friendship, life immediately becomes much more enjoyable. This same principle applies to money: if we are attached to money, we will not be blessed with it. If we part with our attachments and let go of money, simply being generous and thankful for what surrounds us, our financial standing will improve. I admit that it is easier for good, honest people to put these things into practice; but I also believe that even the most selfish person will come to understand these deep truths through the secret teachings of Himalayan esotericism.

Creatively Starting Again

Looking at television and newspaper reports, we often see news of flooding in many parts of the world. Water has a terrifying power, capable of washing everything away. Flooding is tragic for those who are victims of it; however, if we take a more distanced view, we see that, for the natural world, it has a balancing effect. The powerful energy of water cleans everything; through flooding, everything is washed and cleansed.

Humans, too, through their karma, have destroyed nature, and created an artificial nature in its place. But nature continues to balance itself, through climate change, flooding, etc. This is a warning from nature: it is necessary for all of us to give up our obsessions and desires, and embrace living in awareness. The path to inner, personal peace will give us the power to change the environment.

Yes, loss is painful, and the losses I am suggesting here are considerable. However, our hearts must be able to accept great changes if we are to usefully start again with a clean slate. It sounds harsh, I know, but even such disasters as floods can be thought of as opportunities in which to reflect on the mind and break free of its attachments. If we remain attached to old things, we cannot proceed to what is next. It is important to register crises as challenges and be prepared to creatively start again.

The same can be said about the workplace. People despair if the company they work for goes bankrupt, but this is not the way they ought to respond. Again, I would like people to try to view such events as opportunities for a new start. If we think about things this way, we will be better able to see the light to go on. Disasters, then, are certainly setbacks, but perhaps they also serve to bring us better things.

How would you feel if you knew that, starting today, you would no longer have food? Most people would panic immediately. But such a circumstance would never make Yogis—practitioners of Yoga—depressed. Under these conditions, they would switch their thinking and consider the lack of food as an opportunity to rest their internal organs, a chance to rejuvenate their essence. Most of us, I am sure, would be afraid, and obsess over the fact that we may die if we don't eat for several days. This mental unease—this fear—produces toxins in the body that circulate through it and weaken it.

If you can be grateful, with a peaceful mind, you will come to regard setbacks as opportunities and the end results will be beneficial rather than harmful.

Change Is an Opportunity for Thanks

Illness is also a good opportunity to reexamine ourselves. In many cases, people who suffer from illness had been living well until they fell ill. The body or mind may have been sending the message that "it's dangerous to continue like this," but, for whatever reason, the person wasn't able to hear it. Because they continued to press on in the same way, the body was pushed to its limit and the person became ill. Again, we can learn from the times when we are ill. Indeed, illness presents us with an opportunity to study ourselves and to be thankful, and perhaps to become aware of who we really are.

Disasters are times of change as well as opportunities for thanks. When you become ill, try not to be anxious but, instead, think of your illness as a useful change that is restoring a necessary balance. Try to accept it with gratitude. People who habitually worry, even about the immediate future, amplify their anxiety when they become ill. When this happens, the mind receives additional negative energy; not only does the illness linger, but the person's life force is weakened, which further exacerbates their condition.

Strange though it may seem, the important attitude to have in times of illness is one of gratitude. Of course, I am not suggesting that it is unnecessary to seek medical advice, have your condition correctly diagnosed, and take the appropriate course of action. But I do urge you not to have negative thoughts about your illness. This is not about comparing yourself with others; it is about throwing away the mind that desires a return to health.

The secret teachings of the Himalayan Siddha masters are teachings of practices that cleanse the body, senses, and mind, rebalancing them and restoring them from the true source. Samadhi Yoga is unification with God, and *Anugraha*—which we will discuss later—has the power to heal all things. What is unnatural falls away, and we return to a state of original balance. This is where the miracle of healing takes place.

It is good to be thankful for all things and to live a life in accordance with the truth, without focusing on getting better or worrying too much. Your illness has presented you with an opportunity to study, and the object of study is yourself. Learn to coexist with illness and improve yourself from it; eventually your life force will increase, and you will overcome what ails you. Then, you will become your true self. There is no illness there.

Difficult Times Are Also Chances for Learning

Disaster and illness are not the only opportunities for change. Difficulties in personal relationships, both at work and at home, are also good opportunities to examine ourselves and make changes.

I had one woman consult me about this. She was distressed because of her inability to get rid of feelings of anger toward a junior coworker and feelings of discontent about the way a senior coworker was acting: "I have a lot of work experience. I'm able to do a much better job than my junior coworker, but the senior coworker only gives opportunities to her. I'm so frustrated I can hardly stand it. What should I do?" At times like this it is always best to look inside ourselves rather than blame the other party. If we do this, we may find that there is insufficient love, gratitude, wisdom, or understanding there.

Favoritism and unfairness often create difficult situations in the workplace, but these, too, present opportunities for change in the same way as disaster and illness. Rather than feeling troubled, it is better to be grateful that an opportunity has presented itself, allowing us to turn and look at ourselves, and to learn from what we see.

When we feel envious or jealous, waves of discomfort are created, our feelings toward others become negative, and our feelings toward ourselves suffer as well. The mind attracts things of the same nature and resists things of a different nature. It often happens that, if you think you dislike someone, they will begin to dislike you. Such situations involve the mind operating at a very low level of awareness. In order to rise above this, it is crucial to trust ourselves more. If we praise the growth of others and do what we should be doing at any given moment, we too will grow, and our good actions will soon be noticed by others.

Gratitude for Being in Difficult Circumstances

If we look at things this way, we will come to understand that illness and argument, accident and disaster, division between relations and friends, and even bankruptcy and loss of work all look like misfortune but are actually learning opportunities. Even things that cause us substantial inconvenience present us with learning opportunities. Trials and tribulations, then, are opportunities for learning that can help us to cleanse and change ourselves—they are not necessarily bad things.

What if life was easy and only nice things happened to us? We would live peacefully but without growing as human beings. It is precisely because there are unpleasant and difficult experiences in our lives that we are able to deeply examine ourselves. So, too, if everyone around us was always agreeable, we would struggle to be able to see ourselves. When we meet with those who think differently or those we don't like, or with disagreeable circumstances, a shadow that isn't normally seen—called karma—floats to the surface. We will talk about this later. Even if, right now, you are in a situation so difficult you feel as though you would rather lie down on a bed of nails, please try to find it in your heart to give thanks.

I cannot overemphasize how important it is to examine such circumstances. Who or what is feeling the pain? Is it you or your mind? Reactive mind, the mind that reacts and responds to your environment, is part of the shadow inside you. Over time, you will become aware of this. And later, through meditation training, you will come to see so much more. The Sanskrit word for "see" is *drasta*; becoming able to see is called *bawa*. Deepening awareness and attaining enlightenment is *drasta bawa*.

Through deepening awareness you will come to know your true self, which is the release from suffering. Then, an exciting new path will unfurl in front of you.

Having Love and Cleansing Negative Thoughts

We all know people who are prone to saying unreasonable things. There are probably one or two people around you who, from time to time, say malicious things. But, if you happen to be on the receiving end of this type of speech or behavior, please don't think of yourself as the victim. Rather than taking the path of negative awareness, by talking back or trying to injure the other person, choose the path of love and forgiveness. This is compassion. If you are able to practice compassion, even in the little things, your life will change considerably.

I have encountered many people who are unable to put these words into practice. "If that's the way it is, I'm the one who loses. Why am I the only one who must forgive? You have to fight, if someone brings the fight to you!" We think this way because our minds are habituated to calculating losses and gains. But we can't move forward this way. We have to let go of this kind of thinking.

You must meet the person who is being mean to you with trust and love. Take the situation as an opportunity for study and employ gratitude and forgiveness. People are connected at a deep level, and the kindness of your forgiveness will be conveyed to the other person at this deep level, instigating change. You will change, and so will the other person. Let love heal your pain. By loving yourself, the negative thoughts inside you will be cleansed, and understanding and love for others will grow. Please try, in earnest, not to forget love, and strive to forgive those around you, rather than find fault.

Those who are sick often unconsciously voice discontent as a result of fixating on getting well. When this happens, toxins are released in the body, which slow recovery. If, on the other hand, a person who is sick feels a deep sense of gratitude for the tiniest improvement in their condition, they will heal faster.

Many people set their sights on what they lack, be it money or kindness or whatever; do they notice how wonderful the day was, or how fortunate they are to live every day in safety and good health? We tend to be thankful only for external things, but there are blessings we cannot see for which we should also be thankful.

3

All Outcomes Are Created by Your Mind: If You Desire Something, It Can Be Realized

Don't Be Bound by Meaningless Rules

In society, there are unspoken rules and conventions that are known as "common sense"—eat three meals a day, sleep for eight hours a night, etc. In a natural environment, if we lived according to our intuition, we would eat when we wanted to eat, and sleep as much as we needed to, when we needed to. But perhaps, then, when we wanted to eat, we would eat too much—perhaps it's for the best that we live in a fairly well-regulated way. However, when we create such rules, they quickly become absolutes, and we find ourselves bound by them, hand and foot.

It is often claimed that not eating three meals a day is unhealthy, but is that really true? Up through the Edo period in Japan, it was normal to eat two meals a day. Certainly, three meals may help to spread out our intake of nutrients, but today there are many people for whom mealtimes are simply a source of excess calories and the cause of various diseases. In modern Japan, there are many times when we think, "We have to do this," or, "If we don't do that we'll fall behind the times!" If we really thought about it, we would see that they are all unnecessary things, but we are always too busy to really think.

There are people who feel ill if they don't shower and wash their hair every morning, but this is nothing more than a subjective impression. In the Edo period, there was no such thing as a shower. Of course, as our lifestyles change, so do our habits. Today, as much as the world is overflowing with material things and modern conveniences, so, on the other hand, has the number of things that we "must" do grown. We are shackled to these everyday meaningless rules, and we feel we have to do this thing or that thing, or else, with the result that we never feel as though we have enough time. Our trivial to-do list takes priority, and that which is truly essential gets erased. And so we live our lives with our minds in a constant state of turmoil, and with no time for self-reflection. Don't let your mind be taken over by meaningless rules!

The Trick to Making Living Easy

It is important, of course, to avoid making mistakes, and it is healthy to live a well-regulated life. However, it is also the case that many people try to observe convention to such a degree that they become unnecessarily anxious and nervous, and completely unable to live simply.

People who obsess over health and dieting are, in fact, good examples of people who are unable to live simply. They punish themselves for eating a little too much or for snacking without thinking and end up with their priorities reversed. This is wrong. To throw off the various entrapments and imprisonments of life and accept your true self is far more important. Through Himalayan Yoga, you can deepen your attention, free the mind of its imprisonments, and get in touch with what is truly important. If we thought logically about how surrounded we are by things we could easily do without, we would be utterly dumbfounded. But, because we hold onto these things and are unable to let them go, we fail to recognize our suffering.

Haven't our lives become excessively complicated? Let's take a single kitchen utensil as an example. This food goes with that dish, this pot, that knife—we possess several almost identical things for every individual meal. As a result, our kitchens overflow with objects and cleanup becomes that much harder. What if we only had one type of dish or pot? Could we not get by? Often, when we buy a convenient piece of cookware, we come to regard it as junk before we have even mastered it. If we had the skill, we could do pretty much everything with a single chef's knife (and save so much space!).

This way of thinking can be applied to all things. If you can think in this way, you can live a comfortable, simple life, free of the confusion caused by unnecessary things.

Know That "My Mind Is Not Me"

Most of us think of ourselves as consisting of our bodies and minds. We hide in their shadows, not believing that there is a soul deep within. In Western culture, discussion of consciousness and the subconscious has largely been based on the works of Freud and Jung. Discussion of self-consciousness, which surpasses the traditional sense of the word "consciousness," and the divine super-consciousness which surpasses that, has only come about in recent times.

By purifying your mind and body, by removing all cloudiness, you can deepen your perception of who you really are. In doing so, the real you appears, and you realize that neither mind nor body is truly the real you. Our true forms are not our minds, but something more powerful. Through meditation, you will come to see that our true forms are pieces—offshoots—of the gods. If you can truly know and live this, you will never be sidetracked or misled by your mind, and you will become a person of great love.

The problem is that, over the course of our long relationships with our minds, our minds have been spoiled. They now think they are entirely responsible for running the show, and that they can lead us around by the nose. It is not your family, your acquaintances, or any other external entity that tempts you or leads you astray. It is simply your mind. You must, therefore, believe in yourself and watch your mind very carefully. And, more than this, you must polish and refine your mind until it is pure, and you will become your pure consciousness. Become a person who is able to let go. Don't be enslaved to your mind.

Why You Make the Same Mistakes Over and Over

The mind's energy is strong and acts like a magnet, attracting many things. And the fixations of the mind are tenacious indeed, forcing the same thoughts to come, repeatedly. If we keep the memories of such fixations inside ourselves, even if they concern something unpleasant or hurtful, the next time we find ourselves in a similar situation, the old energies will be stimulated, and we will end up behaving in the same way. That is, the various energies of the past have the power to rule our thoughts and actions in the present. It is because of this, for example, that we change jobs to be rid of a nasty boss, only to find ourselves working for an even more disagreeable person.

The important thing is to approach our relationships with others and our actions in all situations with a mind that is free from obstructive thoughts. Do not hate. Do not fixate. Try to look upon everything with love. If you encounter an inconsiderate, rude, or ungrateful person, try not to judge them. Instead, think to yourself, "That person is acting like that in order to protect themselves. It must be hard for them. Everyone's doing their best in life. I appreciate their efforts." Work to purify your mind. Release it from its usual chains.

The Mind Draws Unhappiness and Disaster as Well

Look within. If you understand what is happening inside you, you will come to be aware of this truth: whatever we think, within ourselves, can be given shape and allowed to materialize in the external world. Getting sick, meeting with disaster or accident, falling out with someone close, the company going bankrupt—we feel that such things are externally motivated and befall us for reasons beyond our control. No. The force that brings about these events is the self. This is what is called karma.

Karma contains good and bad and exists in various types. There is the karma that is produced from our memory of the results of our actions since birth. There is also the karma that comes from our memory of our actions from before our birth. The results of the karma of a person's real actions, as well as their thoughts and spoken actions become memory, become the basis for their next karma. Where karma is concerned, things of a like nature will always attract. If you hold hate within your mind, it will call other hateful things to itself. If you hold fear within your mind, you will misunderstand everything as frightful, call frightful things to yourself, and engender a kind of panic; adrenaline-like hormones will be released, and your body's defense systems will act to protect your body. Some sort of breakdown is often the result.

Because karma behaves in this way, it is vital that you move to purify your inner karma by doing good actions and thinking good thoughts. If you can do this, natural and good things will be called to you, and cause good things to happen. It is not an overstatement to say that purifying one's karma is one of the most important actions you can take in your life; it will improve your quality as a person.

If a person lacks awareness, they live at the mercy of their karma, which does not hesitate to push them around. Karma manifests differently for different people.

For some, it manifests in the head; for others, it targets the stomach. Some people's blood pressure goes up; some people feel it in their nerves, their emotions, or uterus; others have stomachaches, etc. The type of manifestation depends on the kind of person.

The danger comes when the mind acquires a habit from karma: even if it is something harmful to the mind or body, we end up repeating it. This behavior then sets the scene for all manner of misfortunes—depression, disease, disaster. You can use the secret teachings of Himalayan esotericism to avoid being thrown around by such a mind—that is, you can use them to purify your karmic memory. Awareness is crucial; it enables us to separate from our karma and return to ourselves.

The Mind's Habit of Blaming Other People

We often blame others for our mistakes and shortcomings. When we suffer, we blame our parents, our schools, society, the company we work for, or whoever is conveniently to hand. We think external causes are at the root of our suffering and we habitually lash out. But what is painful? And what is pain? If we truthfully pursue that which has caused us to suffer, we will realize that it is not, in fact, the actions of another person.

Actually, many of us recognize, if only at some remote level, that the causes of our actions lie within ourselves; the problem is, we find it easier to blame other people and external factors. Our ignorance obscures our vision, and we find that we like things this way—they are easier. We balance and protect ourselves by putting the responsibility on others.

What we ought to be doing is retuning our minds to give them good habits. Reeducating our minds, in other words. In doing so, we can achieve harmony and become our true selves. Then, no matter how trying the circumstances, we can help others, and be able to forgive and love. But we must understand the truth. Associating with unbalanced people who do not believe in themselves causes our own karma to be affected: if we try to send good karma their way, it is only at the level of the ego, and it has the negative effect of drawing out the other person's ego and wrapping us in it, so that we end up embroiled in the same negativity.

Change the Mind and Its Surroundings Will Also Change

Our consciousness is focused outward and is overdeveloped in that regard; we equate the outside world with reality. However, we must not forget that the *internal* is the source from which the external world is created. I truly mean this: it is our minds that create all things.

By looking at our minds, we can understand why we have chosen a particular course of action. By purifying our minds and deepening our awareness, our unfettered status—our true selves—will appear externally. Conversely, when the mind is encumbered by a miscellany of thoughts or with feelings of dissatisfaction, anger, or hatred, we remain clouded and unaware.

While our minds remain unchanged, no matter how much we try to change the outside world, everything will remain the same. If we change what is within us, then others will change, and so will our surrounding environment. If you change yourself, the reality that surrounds you can also change dramatically.

In Himalayan esotericism, the master who performs the initiation of *diksha* with cleansing waves of secret meditation is able to impart feelings of joy: "Thanks to you, we found an unexpected chance for our family to talk. I had no particular intention to do so, but I was able to speak to my father, who I have not gotten along with for forty years. It was the first time we had talked since I married my husband. As a result, my father and I made plans to travel with our family for my brother's childbirth celebration. My father and I both cried, reached a deeper understanding, and our family was united." Thus it was that a mind obstinate in its prejudice against the father was led naturally, through the practice of meditation and the diksha of Himalayan Yoga, to a joyful reconciliation.

The mind becomes pure; nature, love, and forgiveness abound, and, even if there was no intent to change the outside world, others and one's surroundings will change of their own accord. If we do this, then improved human relations are a given. Even a mind full of prejudice can be changed by the practice of Himalayan Yoga; it can eventually transcend, become its true self, and free itself of all limitations. A change of mind is a fundamental change indeed, but transcendence of the mind is a complete jump to the other side, the side of total freedom.

Think That the Head Does Not Exist

In order to know truth, it may be better to think that the head doesn't exist. If the head works too hard, it worries about unnecessary things and causes unnecessary suffering. When I was a student, I was told, "Use your brain." It was explained to me that using your head was the smart thing to do, and I worried that, if I didn't use my head, it would somehow go bad.

In the spiritual world there is a saying: "To know the truth is to grow smarter." However, this is not a worldly sort of intelligence. By making the truth your own, you will be able to perceive everything more deeply and naturally, without being a slave to intelligence or anything else. Any murkiness—doubt, confusion—that surrounds the mind and body will vanish, everything will become clear, and the real you will emerge. In other words, by not using your head needlessly, you are better able to understand everything.

This is important. If you purify your head and mind and allow them to become empty, your inherent skills will bloom. I know we have become uncomfortable with not using our heads for long periods of time but doing so is crucial if you are to become the real you. We have the mistaken presumption that our mind is something that evolves as we use it; we find it very hard to accept the idea of *not* using it.

But how great would it be if you could turn your head "off"? Things would become clear and your life energy would begin to accumulate. Your intuition would sharpen and your creativity increase. Unfortunately, in our contemporary reality, the mind is confused. Even when we think we're not using it, it is being used unnecessarily and our life energy is spilling out and going to waste.

This is why, in Yoga, we do not supply energy: we control it. Also, we control our minds, and practice stopping up all the "holes" from which energy could leak: our nostrils, our earholes, our anuses. Of course, this is Yoga at quite an advanced level; at the beginning, we think of holes simply as outlets that allow us to expel toxins and purify the self.

Empty Your Mind, Let Go of the Ego

If you are to achieve enlightenment, you must cleanse and beautify your mind and body from within, make them empty, and let go of your ego in its entirety. Do not think with your head. Feel the laws of energy, and, through your perception, live freely.

We humans are born from the fundamental—that is, the divine—and made to live through love, wisdom, and power. We can think of the modern age as nothing more than an arrogant mind that functions to weaken these bonds. Many of us forget our true selves, even our fundamental existence, and do nothing but complain about life and society.

To remedy this situation, you must turn your consciousness toward the true self and toward the fundamental existence, bow your head, and offer up sincere gratitude. "I am devoted to you, I can put my ego to rest for a time," is a good thing to say when you do so. As your meditation practice advances, you will be bathed in energy from top to bottom like a flowing river and may find both your mind and physical body healed. A doubtful heart or selfish pride will prevent love, wisdom, and power from coming. Prejudice and greed will also cause them to slip away. If you are full of such things, you will be unable to feel the flow of positive energies.

If You Ask for It, It Can Be Granted

Let's take a closer look at the question, "What is truth?" If we look closely at our true selves, we will come to know our minds and bodies fully, which will allow us to surpass them and return to a state of simply being. This is what it means to become your true self. This is because we are all our own little universes within the greater universe in which everything exists. And so we return to the fundamental existence that produces each little universe. Again, this is the true self, an offshoot of the divine. Look toward your true self with trust, give life to everything, and truly experience the fundamental existence that is the divine.

The breathing method introduced in Chapter Two that uses the life energy of prana is also born of the fundamental existence, the divine. When you join the divine, those wishes that would not come true, no matter how much you tried, will do so. The divine is the existence that created everything. As you progress along the path to becoming your true self, your ties to this existence will grow stronger, and, as your power increases, your prayers will begin to be answered. In becoming divine, the body and mind are purified, and, as your potential increases, your desires melt away.

To become divine is to become the ocean. Here, a river loses its meaning. Rivers flow into the ocean and become one.

Traditionally, when we talk of gods, we envisage a far-off and elevated existence. The secret teachings of Himalayan Yoga have torn away this veil. Through them, you can step onto the path to your true self and even become one with the divine.

There Is Wisdom, Power, and Love

By ridding yourself of obstructive thoughts and deepening your awareness, you will be able to understand what is important. This, in turn, will increase your potential to seize chances for success in both your personal and professional life. All of your knowledge and skills, which have gone to waste up until now, will be given full license and put to the best possible use.

Rid the mind of thoughts that simply get in your way! Clear all the junk out of there! If you can create an empty space in your mind, you will be able to receive wisdom and power from the fundamental existence that is the divine. If you know the rules of energy, are connected by unconditional love, and have faith in the source of existence, you will encounter limitless power. You will be led in the right direction, able to develop your skills and creativity, and have your very life force strengthened. Everything will quickly come to fulfillment, all that you have wished for will be yours, and your dreams will be realized.

The more you purify your heart, the more your power will mature. If you can cast aside your attachments to outward appearance and be clear of obtrusive thoughts, if you can humbly dedicate yourself to living in purity, you will be able to focus your willpower and identify your goals, direct your energy toward them, and fulfill your dreams. Furthermore, if you desire for nothing, you will become free, and able to gain anything.

Eventually, you will arrive at a place of zero energy expenditure. You will become your true self and achieve the ultimate goal of becoming one with the divine.

Yagya and Diksha, Meditation That Grants Wishes

By becoming your true self, you will become your own master. You will overflow with love, well up with wisdom, and succeed, in every meaning of the word. It is the teachings of Himalayan esotericism that make this possible, that bring it about. The mind becomes empty and joins with the ultimate existence that is the divine and becomes nothingness itself. You will reach the source where anything and everything return to nothingness. Nothingness is the mother of everything; it gives us good fortune, peace, and grants success to all our actions. Please put your faith in nothingness! By looking to nothingness, you can live the life you want.

Also, believe in yourself and live with perception, and consideration for others. For the purification of karma, the *Yagya* prayer ceremony may be helpful; this is similar to the Japanese *gomataki*, in which cedar sticks are burned in prayer for blessings. Energy waves are crucial—they are strong and will naturally lead you to success. A master or guru will give cleansing instruction on samadhi power, as well as the energy waves for success.

Creative meditation for success is also effective. In this, with an unobstructed heart, clearly imagine what it is you want to be, what it is you want to have. This is *shinkui* (action, speech, and thought), the three-in-one action. Through this process, your dreams will be fulfilled. However, this is still the work of the mind. You will eventually surpass your mind and aim for the highest enlightenment: *moksha*, or perfect freedom—enlightenment that can be put to practical use.

4

The Path I Walked: Training in the Himalayas, and Achievement of Samadhi

The Grace of the Himalayas

The seven thousand to eight thousand-meter Himalayan mountain range is said to be home to the divine. Even if you drove for days, you would still find yourself in the mountains. It is a cold land of thin air, covered in glaciers, where the towering, beautiful wilderness stretches out, and one cannot help but be filled with awe and fear. It possesses a beauty that surpasses the season-by-season tastes of humans: snow, rocks, stones, and a blue sky that stretches as far as the eye can see.

In such an environment, if humans are to live, they must develop their minds and bodies to their limits. As opposed to our convenient, modern world, in the car-less Himalayas, one must walk, even if it takes days. The legs develop their traditional sturdiness, the eyes are soothed by looking upon the far-reaching scenery, and the ears hear the usually unheard sounds of the wind and the murmuring of streams. Then, in addition to the sounds of the environment, the natural sounds which come from within, otherwise known as the inner nada, can be heard, and even the sound of microscopic life becomes audible over time.

There is no shortage of sages living in caves, but the Himalayas are about as expansive as Japan. Within this area are unexplored regions of hinterland with no means of access, and continuous, uninhabitable plains at altitudes of over four thousand to five thousand meters. Finding a place suitable for meditation or meeting with an enlightened sage is an extremely difficult task.

However, I have had the good fortune to meet Himalayan sages and have been allowed to succeed in samadhi. Samadhi, translated as "immersion," surpasses space and time, and is the way to become your true self, and join with the divine. It goes beyond life, beyond death. There is no need to go anywhere. You are there now. You can control your life force and return to the origin. Through the grace of the Himalayan gurus, I was able to experience a truly extreme samadhi, and receive wisdom and comprehension.

Memories of Childhood

Before speaking of my Himalayan experience, I will simply introduce how I first encountered yoga, and how I experienced the wisdom of the Himalayan sages that is Himalayan Yoga.

In the Japan of my childhood, the economy had not yet developed, and people still wore geta, or wooden sandals. There were umbrellas, but they were made of paper—when it rained, the streets became filled with mud, which would splatter and soil your clothes. However, since we all lived that way, no one felt especially poor; it was an uncomplicated time. In summer, people would cool themselves on benches in their *yukata* and the old men in the neighborhood could be seen walking around the water-sprinkled streets in their underwear.

When I was very young, I was apparently a very spiritually attuned child. In kindergarten I was always nice to what we would now call the bullied children. As far as I was concerned, there was no feeling of wanting to help another child who seemed pitiful, but there was a strong feeling of wanting *everyone* to be happy, and so I acted accordingly. My father passed away when I was only one and a half years old, so perhaps my behavior was a way of compensating for a lack in my heart.

As I played with the children of other families, I thought it strange that parents were not affectionate toward any children but their own. From that perception, I grew up with the vague thought that one should love everyone equally.

Here is a story from my third grade year. During a typhoon with winds of forty-five meters per second, the door of our house was ripped off. However, my older brother, who was older than me by fourteen years, was a member of the fire department and had left the house because the weir was about to burst its banks. In the house at the time were my two older sisters (four years and seven years older), my mother, and me, all women. It was a wooden house, so when the strong winds began blowing through the house we all thought the ceiling and roof were going to be blown right off. My older sisters were in a panic, crying, "What should we do? What should we do?" It was a split-second judgment that led me, the youngest one in the house, to say, "Hey! Pick up those bamboo mats and bring the boards over here!" I took the initiative, crossed the boards, and, with hammer and nails, closed up the doorway.

We were all relieved, and everyone kept complimenting me, saying how amazing and steadfast I was and how brave my actions were.

The Walking Race When I Was in Junior High School

In junior high school, during physical education class, we competed against each other in groups, but I didn't find it enjoyable. Even in basketball, if you weren't strong or sufficiently strong-willed, you couldn't steal the ball from others or interfere with their passes. I wasn't very good at these kinds of sports.

I was a nonathletic child, but I remember the walking race during my first year of junior high. It was a competition that started at four o'clock in the morning and involved walked over the various mountains in the Koushuu area. I was walking along, talking at length with my friends, when, perhaps because of weariness, one of them, then two of them, disappeared, and somehow I found myself with nobody around me. I was plodding along, crossing the Daibosatsu pass alone, when a group of women started to cheer me on. Sometime later, perhaps several hours later, I finally made it back to my school. Just when I was thinking that everyone else must have left for the day and that I was surely the last one back, I heard a cry of "First one!" I was shocked. I had never really done any physical training, but I walked to and from school every day, so maybe that had something to do with it. In the actions of my everyday life, my legs and pelvis had been toughened, which gave me some measure of strength. The walking race was certainly a case of "where there's a will, there's a way." This event had a huge impact on me.

The Words I Said to My Mother One Day

At school, I didn't study with any great passion, but I didn't suffer through it either—I enjoyed it, on the whole. I was never scolded, and I did what came naturally to me. Relatives and neighbors praised me and called me good. I think I was what we call a low-maintenance child. However, I do remember one occasion when I behaved unreasonably. My father became ill due to overwork, and I remember my mother telling my older sister, "A child who studies won't become a bride." One day, I said, " I am not going to become a bride, so please just give me money!" I wanted the money to buy a book, but I knew that, if I simply asked for the money, I would have been yelled at. I remember exactly how I felt, as soon as I had said these words. I had said what I wanted to say, and I felt very relaxed and happy. I had, without realizing it, learned that there is great comfort to be had in giving voice to and clearly stating one's thoughts.

My Encounter with Yoga

During my first summer vacation in high school, after a very intense foray into the study of cuisine, my face was covered in a rash. At that time, I was highly susceptible to stress, and bad things would happen, not so much back-to-back as all at once. This was the impetus for my looking into health food, which, in those days, was still a highly unusual topic, and for attending and practicing at a fasting retreat.

From that point on, I developed an interest in health and hygiene and read many books on it. During my reading, I encountered something called yoga, and devoted myself to the study of the mind and body. My college years were a time of student movements and protests, but, even when my college was closed, I continuously studied yoga.

Perhaps the greatest appeal of yoga is that, unlike muscle training or sports, it energizes without depleting one's stamina. Yoga helps the entire body to achieve balance, naturally removes the body's distortions, and has an incredible effect on the stomach, intestines, and internal organs in general. For someone like me, with very little physical stamina, sports that require you to match your partner's pace or strategy are difficult. Because I could do yoga at my own pace, and because it felt so good, I came to like it.

Even so, the difficult poses were troublesome. For example, a famous pose in yoga, the kurmasana, or turtle pose, involves dropping your rear end, throwing your legs out in front, and arranging the whole body in the shape of a turtle. An acquaintance of mine who is very flexible was able to do this pose immediately, but for me, in the beginning, it was very difficult: "What do you mean I have to put my legs behind my head?!" But, after a lot of trouble at first, even this pose became fun.

Unfortunately, upon becoming an adult, I experienced a variety of troubles and wasn't able to consistently practice yoga. One day, I had a chest X-ray as part of a regular health checkup, and the doctor found that I had tuberculosis. I had certainly been coughing, but, as I didn't feel so bad overall, I had paid it little mind. I should have paid more attention to the fact that my father died of tuberculosis; perhaps I was also possessed of this trait.

Tuberculosis has two levels, one and two, denoted by the progression of the disease. I remember being admitted to hospital as a very bad case. I was fortunate to be cured, but, for several years afterward, my every move, even my every breath, was filled with fear. Tuberculosis requires complete bed rest and that one not strain one's nerves; it imposes many limitations. Also, they say that when the body is healthy, so is the bug—even moving is frightening.

However, I was able to break through this taboo. I believed in myself and moved on. I became a follower of the divine secrets of yoga and, over time, I recovered and became healthy once again. Then I began to put what I had learned into practice, in earnest. I began to live with yoga.

When I Looked Deep into my Mind

While practicing yoga, something unexpectedly took root in my mind. I started thinking about what our minds are, exactly.

I thought of myself as a good person. I didn't quarrel with other people or possess a malicious temperament. However, when I looked deep within myself, I found a jealous heart, one that got depressed when it lost, one that had desires, always wanting for this or that. At the end of thoroughly investigating this, I came to understand one important fact: the mind creates everything. Everything that befalls you is created in your own mind. It is common to blame other people, your parents, or the environment for things that go wrong. However, if you examine the cause carefully, you will find it's entirely your own fault.

I continued to further my practice and study of yoga, not just from the standpoint of physical well-being, but also of philosophy and religion. Eventually I was invited to teach at a cultural center, and my yoga came to be known as Aikawa Yoga. Because I was teaching, I had to further improve myself, and deepen my own understanding. I studied breath control and dance and began to teach at other cultural centers.

Because I wanted as many people as possible to grow and develop, I started to train other instructors, all the while pushing myself to higher and higher levels. I was convinced that I was in pursuit of the truth, and firmly on the road to enlightenment.

Pursue True Peace of Mind

When I was little, I always asked, "Why? Why?" but nobody would answer me. I continued to learn as best I could, but I always yearned for a great teacher, partly because I would get flustered sitting by myself in front of great, thick books. I continued my studies, but I did not know peace of mind.

Zen Buddhism was attractive to me, and I traveled to India every year to meditate at various Yoga retreats. My body grew stronger, which, in itself, made me happy, and things began to go the way I wanted. However, even though I was becoming successful, I still constantly questioned myself: What should I do to make others happier? What did I need to do to become a better leader? What kind of person did I need to become, if I was to love everybody?

I was traveling constantly—to New York, California, London—and learning various forms of New Age healing, along with psychological and physical therapies. These are all boom industries in Japan today, but, twenty-five years ago, those who were interested had to travel far and wide if they were to encounter like-minded souls. In the United States, anything can be turned into a business, and I experienced many "spirituality on parade" events. Also, there were as many forms of psychotherapy as there were practitioners. I met many people, who, despite professing to know everything, seemed only to invite more confusion.

I continued my travels and continued my search for answers to my questions. Eventually, I was rewarded with the chance to meet a great Himalayan guru.

The Himalayan Guru Pilot Babaji

In November 1984 I was approached by a Japanese TV station that had invited a Himalayan guru, Pilot Babaji, to perform a public samadhi in Tokyo. The station requested my assistance as a yoga teacher. Pilot Babaji is the supreme leader of the Indian spiritual world. He is sought after like a living Buddha and has performed more than one hundred public samadhis. Now he was to hold an underground samadhi in Tokyo, to demonstrate truth to the Japanese people.

Pilot Babaji entered into an underground cave, completely cut off from the outside world, and performed a deep, four-day samadhi. Then, once he had become one with the divine, he returned. This underground samadhi is the ultimate practice in Yoga and demonstrates that one has become a bright, immortal soul. In India, those who perform underground samadhis are respected and revered as great sages. Only those few sages who live deep within the Himalayas can attain this highest state; the exquisite samadhi energy they release purifies and heals the people of the earth.

After the TV program had been filmed, Pilot Babaji invited me to the Himalayas. I had long dreamed of making a visit to this holy land, and I immediately accepted. While the Himalayas is well known as the region where great sages practice the secret science of life, it remains a vast place with a forbidding geography and climate. It is a very dangerous place to visit, without the guidance of one who knows it well.

Also, this was no simple adventure, but a spiritual journey on which I was to undergo rigorous training. I had been to and practiced in the sacred regions of Haridwar and Rishikesh, but I had never ventured into the Himalayan wilderness, those areas deeper in the mountains such as Gangotri and Gaumukh. The prospect set my heart to fluttering.

It was an extraordinary stroke of luck to have met Pilot Babaji in Japan. He was a great sage who lived and practiced in the Himalayan interior. He had achieved samadhi and he lived a true life.

The Journey to the Himalayas: The Place from the Ramayana

The Himalayas are wondrous: world-famous for their beauty, and home to a hidden science, where spiritual power abounds. There are many sages who meditate there in scattered, hidden places. Some are praying to their gods, others are in samadhi. The area's history extends back to ancient times, five to ten thousand years ago, and there are thousands of secret shrines.

My journey began with training in Sattar. After acclimating my body, I set my sights on a journey to the even more secluded Pindali Glacier. This was the path into Tibet and considered a wild region. I enlisted the help of a local guide and we set out. The journey to Pindali would take three days by car from New Delhi, followed by several days of walking. The area had, at one time, been completely sealed off, and totally unexplored.

After setting out from New Delhi, we first arrived at the sacred area of Bageshwar, where there are old temples and the air feels thick with memories of spiritual power. The riverbank that can be seen from the ashram, a training studio and temple, is a historical site that features in the five-thousand-year-old legend of the Ramayana. In the ashram I met many sages, but I was most impressed by a venerated, nearly hundred-year-old Babaji named Barkrishna Maharaj, who was also a philosopher and had traveled to Mount Kailash.

On the third day of our journey, we arrived at a small village called Song, and, from there, we continued on foot. Walking along the rugged Sarayu river one day, we happened to meet the sage Narayan Swami. He was about 142 years old and lived constantly in meditation. I remember his beautifully shining white hair and my impression of him as a wise figure. He spoke to me about the Himalayas and other sages.

We continued walking and passed many villages. We climbed, making paths for ourselves where there were no paths. Sometimes we walked, and sometimes we rode horses. Four days after our departure from Song, we arrived at Pindali.

Beautiful Scenery and Plain Faith

It was May 1985, and I was finally standing in the secluded Pindari gorge, said to be the most beautiful and dangerous part of the Himalayas. I kept thinking to myself, "I must be dreaming." Before my eyes was a panorama of the eight-thousand-meter-high mountains of the Himalayas. In the vicinity were numerous caves and small cottages made from stones. We went to a place roughly thirty minutes' walk from the Pindari Glacier.

On top of the cave was a small temple built by Pilot Babaji, made of small stones stacked on top of one another. I offered prayers and rested. The snowmelt waters of the Pindari Glacier and Nanda Devi mountains form the source for many rivers. One of these is the Pindar River that runs alongside Mount Matri. On top of the Pindari Glacier, the eight-thousand-plus-meter peaks of Nanda Devi, Nanda Kot, and Nanda Kat form a line and are connected to the road into Tibet. At the top of the glacier there are many beautiful lakes. Past the peak of Nanda Devi, the mountains continue. Beyond them is the beautiful Mount Kailas.

Training on Pindari Glacier

The caves in Pindari have been there for many hundreds of millions of years. The energy of all the Himalayan sages who have trained there can be felt. When I came into contact with that energy, I felt that this was not my first time in this place, but that I had been there in one of my past lives. At the same time, a change began within my body. I immediately sat down and entered a deep meditative state.

Up until then, I had spent many years in Japan practicing meditation, spending forty days at a time eating nothing, shut within my room, practicing samadhi. I experienced my body shrinking and growing, even my soul leaving my body and flying around the room. In this way, I gradually closed in on achieving samadhi, step by step. Finally, on my third journey to Pindari, I achieved samadhi. Let me tell you about that experience.

In going to the secluded parts of the Himalayas, I became aware of the fact that the wilderness was welcoming and accepting me. Also, I could feel that my body was changing. I was aware of an outpouring of strength from within me, and I knew that I could continue to sit for a long time. I declared my intentions to Pilot Babaji and the other sages, asked them to guard my surroundings, entered the cave, and sat down.

To enter samadhi, the body must be pure, so you can become free. I prepared my body, reached a state of harmony, and finally my body began to shake. My head felt tight, as if energy was struggling to burst out. I remember pain. My body also began to get extremely hot, as if I had gotten into a hot spring. My legs felt as though they were on fire. I felt like a volcano had erupted and was causing lava to rise up in my body. Then, my whole body was like fire; I began to feel I was no longer human.

Becoming One's True Self in Samadhi

I surpassed my body and mind and got closer to myself. There was no body, no mind, and no cave, and the sky was opening. I continued, deeper and deeper. Suddenly, a tunnel appeared, and I entered. It felt like dying. If I felt that I had a mind, I would probably have turned back, without entering.

But I kept going. I went farther into the dark tunnel, until a limitless, infinite space stretched out before me. Here, I became one with time—I was pure being. In other words, I had become my true self. Around me sat great souls. Jesus Christ was there. Buddha was there. Many great souls were there. All became one, and the soul of enlightenment was there. A sacred soul appeared, and I was within it.

The souls were not people, as such; they were beings. For a very short time, everything was oneness, a harmonious single body, which birthed sacred wisdom. Space opened and distance vanished. I surpassed time. Everything came together. There was no Buddha or Christ; everything was one. There was no past or future; only the present.

When the soul and mind receive the light of wisdom, all knowledge is realized, and one sees great souls—one does not see individuals. These are souls that have received the light: pure beings. I understood that I was with entities that had received the light of wisdom. Everything became one within me—even me. I was not a body. Buddha was within me. Jesus Christ was within me. When everything is the same, there is no comparison. The world that is beyond the mind and the body is also beyond space, time, and even death. It is the world of now. It is samadhi. In samadhi, one gains enlightenment. This whole experience, as recounted here, felt like it took three or so minutes.

Eventually, my consciousness returned from samadhi, and I returned to my mind and body. When the stone blocking the entrance to the cave was removed, I stepped out and was shocked. Outside, in the real world, three whole days had passed. In samadhi, one goes beyond time—neither time nor space exist. People saw my countenance and immediately knew I had achieved samadhi. Everyone was happy, and I was received with respect. I noticed that the Pindari Glacier and surrounding mountains reflected in my eyes were brighter than ever. The beautiful, secluded wilderness of the Himalayas smiled and welcomed me. I walked the mountains and enjoyed my enlightenment.

Enlightenment: An Experience Beyond Death

And so, I had experienced samadhi. Now I thought about how I wanted to communicate this peace to people, how to communicate and nurture truth. I thought about what I could do for people, what I could offer people who are interested in peace and love.

I also felt that I wanted to sit more and receive samadhi, and I mentioned this to Pilot Babaji. He told me about a small shrine he had built, a short distance from the cave, on the other side of the river. The interior of this shrine was very simple: it contained statues deifying Pindali, Kali, and Dattatreya, the first practitioners in the world and the masters of all practitioners, and near the entrance was a very small place to sit. I gazed at the images of the gods, and I felt energy. While that energy was watching over me, I began to practice. This is what is called the Anugraha kriya method.

Energy welled up inside me. I felt as though Mount Everest was inside me. I scaled the mountain over and over, until my body had achieved harmony, and I had gained my core. All of my body's systems had become one. My insides had awoken, and I no longer had a body or senses. Everything melted and became as the sea. Then, a very quiet and deep peace arose. I walked into the sea.

Enlightenment happened. I became one with everything. Everything was with me. I was space. I was light. I was pure existence. I was being. I became the sky and universal consciousness. Everything was divine. Everything was supreme consciousness. Everything was within me.

Distance vanished. Time vanished. Space vanished. Past and future did not exist. I was full of light, like the ocean. I was beyond mind, beyond body, and beyond death.

Samadhi Through Practice and Sankalpa

I became my true self, or *Atman*. Then I began to revive and very slowly woke up from supreme consciousness. I returned to self-consciousness, reason, and to my mind and body. Samadhi had occurred due to my practice and my *sankalpa*—that which grants one's wishes and rewards one's vows. This is the laser-like power, which transcends the mind and body, and is a prayer for godlike willpower. One experiences this trance state as a very short period of time—a matter of minutes. This is how I ended a four-day samadhi.

I was now able to enter samadhi at will. I believed in myself and was able to access creative thought. I was no longer the person that I was; now, I could truly give something useful to people. I was so grateful to the Himalayan masters and sages—grateful for their support, and for allowing me to come this far. Now, I felt able to share enlightenment and the power of Himalayan Anugraha with others.

Searching for the True Master

On the spiritual path, the blessing of a master who will lead you is an absolute necessity. In English, *blessing* usually means a gift of luck from God, but in the secret ways of the Himalayas, it points to the high-dimension energy of grace received from a sage who has reached enlightenment.

We know, of course, that teaching and guidance are often necessary in the course of our lives, whether it be from books, parents, teachers, or friends. And so it is, too, for inner practices and the road to samadhi: a master is indispensable. A sage who makes such knowledge available is called a guru, or spiritual guide. In Hindi, *gu* means darkness and *ru* means light.

However, to meet a master, and have him as your guru, is incredibly difficult. Certainly there are sages who spend decades in samadhi, transcending body, mind, and death, sending their souls outward to travel here and there. They are those wondrous sages called samadhi Yogi, or Siddha masters. In the Himalayan tradition, there is a secret way to reach these stages—Siddha masters do not come down to the fields.

Hari Babaji and Ottar Babaji

One day, on the way to the train station in Pindari, I asked Pilot Babaji, "From whom should I take diksha?" He replied, "For you, a great master is needed. Let's go to my master, Hari Babaji." When I heard this, my heart began to throb. I was about to meet the great sage Hari Babaji!

Hari Babaji was famous throughout India as a Siddha master—this was surely a chance sent from heaven. I later found out that Pilot Babaji thought I had good karma and was a lucky person; he had apparently said, "Not only is she at a high level spiritually, she is very passionate, so I think it best that she receive her blessing directly from a master greater than myself, Hari Babaji."

Hari Babaji had traveled India for thirty years performing samadhi and Yagya, the basis for Japanese *gomataki*, or burning of cedar incense in prayer. Then, having guided people, he left word that he would live in the Himalayas, and has lived in the Nepalese Himalayas for over forty-five years now. Hari Babaji's master is a sage called Ottar Babaji. Hari Babaji was, for a long time, Ottar Babaji's only apprentice. Hari Babaji stayed in the same place because Ottar Babaji ordered him to stay. Ottar Babaji is the most revered Himalayan sage; he received his initiation from the godlike existence that was the Siddha master Narayan and became his Siddha master apprentice.

Meeting the Great Sage Hari Babaji

When you think of a sage, what comes to mind? Perhaps an image of a being who emanates a powerful aura and whose holiness makes it hard to approach? Real Siddha masters are nothing like this. Their faces are the image of naïveté, and they hardly speak. They possess not a trace of ego. They are pure and natural creatures—it is as if existence itself were melted into the space their bodies occupy.

Hari Babaji was incredibly skinny and possessed of a serenity and love like the sea. His eyes were large and filled with a deep glow of kindness. The moment I met him, tears rose unbidden to my eyes, and I was filled with nostalgia and happiness. I intuitively felt that he was one of the masters who had helped me from the shadows. Pilot Babaji explained to Hari Babaji that I had been training in the Himalayas and had come to receive diksha from him. When he said that, Hari Babaji smiled a magnificent, otherworldly smile; he understood that I had the ability to undergo diksha.

Then, without speaking much at all, and without even asking what kind of person I was, he gave me diksha. No matter how many questions I asked, he graciously and warmly answered them one by one, and my tears flowed freely from sheer emotion. Hari Babaji explained to me about love and peace; then he granted me the direct grace of the divine Anugraha.

In this way, and with rare fortune, I was able to become a member of the Himalayan family. Normally it is incredibly difficult to receive diksha from a grand Himalayan master. Many people go to the Himalayas, but few indeed are able to meet a Siddha master. Only those who are born with pure hearts and have good karma, or those who have incredibly good karma on merit, are given diksha from a master.

Hari Babaji said to me, "There are people who can receive the grace of the divine Anugraha. You are one of those people."

Testimonial: She Performed Many Miracles
from a seventh-grade student in Tokyo

Since I was little, I have seen many of Yogmata's miracles happen around me and experienced some myself.

When I was in elementary school, one of my classmates would say nasty things, and for a while I hated going to school. My mother and father worried, and suggested I see Yogmata. When I consulted Yogmata, she told me, "Pray that person finds happiness," and gave me a mantra. I then returned home and chanted the mantra, and prayed. The next day, when I went to school, that classmate didn't say anything nasty. From then on, he stopped saying nasty things, we began to play at each other's houses, and both our teachers and classmates were shocked.

In addition to miracles of the mind, Yogmata has performed miracles of the body for me as well. I once broke a bone when I fell in the playground; I immediately went to Yogmata to receive her power. The hospital doctor was very confused: "That's strange! You heal very quickly!"

Yogmata also performed a miracle for my friend. One of my old friends, T, suddenly and for no apparent reason suffered a brain hemorrhage, and his parents were told there was no hope for recovery. Even though he was the same age as me, he couldn't go to school and I thought he would spend the rest of his life unconscious in hospital. It was a shock. I was attending a prayer group with Yogmata at the time, so I decided to pray for T. About a week later, I heard from T's mother that he had miraculously recovered and would be able to return to school the following week. It was quite a revelation and I thought Yogmata was amazing.

Now I really enjoy school. My friends are interesting, classes are fun, and the cultural and sports events are great. If I have a problem, I believe in my heart that, if I ask Yogmata, it can be solved. Thanks to Yogmata, I feel secure and protected, and able to live each day with the confidence and knowledge that, no matter what, everything is okay. I am so grateful that I was able to meet such a serene existence when I was so young.

Diksha Awakens the Inner Self and Changes That Person's Fate

Diksha, or initiation, is an amazing discipline and lesson that allows you to awaken your inner self while receiving energy from a master. If you receive diksha from a master at a very high level, it can help amazing things happen in your life.

A person's body is a universe and the entire universe is contained therein. However, if that person doesn't know their true self and attempts to develop their mind, they will be pushed around by their mind, and fully controlled by it. The human body is a powerful thing that has incredible abilities, but most of us are unaware of this: we live in a more or less unconscious state and know nothing about our true selves. We are trapped by our egos, our heads full of knowledge and ideas gleaned from others—knowledge and ideas which dominate and control us.

However, those who have received diksha can remove themselves from such traps, feel the magnificence of nature, and open their eyes. Diksha links your true self and your master: the power of the universe flows in, and your body and mind are cleansed and awakened. But, if you are to receive a good destiny, preparation is necessary. To receive diksha, it is first necessary to deepen perception and purify the mind and body through positive thoughts and actions. Then, by believing you can meet a high-level master, you will be able to meet one.

I am busy initiating people in diksha throughout Japan. From newborn babies to people over ninety, people are receiving diksha from me, and living under my protection.

The Grace Anugraha

My meeting with Hari Babaji was my final stop; it was my karma. Having received the blessing of the divine and my master, I was purified from within and gifted with wisdom. The blessing I received is called Anugraha and is a favor that can only be granted by a master who has achieved samadhi. The inner self is awakened, altered, and karma is changed and further evolved.

The Nepalese Himalayas are very spiritual and peaceful. Practitioners don't recognize borders, so Mount Kailas, on the other side of the Himalayas, is also blessed by great sages. Throughout this wondrous land, many samadhi Yogi sages have come and gone, and there are those who practice still. Hari Babaji is one of them, as is his guru, Ottar Babaji. I have been tremendously lucky: to be surrounded by my Himalayan family is a feeling that is impossible to forget.

The great value of diksha can be hard to understand, especially for those of us who live in so-called advanced societies. I experienced a true diksha and I have a good understanding of why it is important. There are truly incredible disciplines and invaluable lessons contained within it. Such is its power, that it helps a person to awaken internally and gives them a new life.

Again, I must emphasize the impossibility of proceeding without a guide—the grace of a Siddha master is crucial. A real samadhi experience will change the mind and body and being able to transcend these is another benefit of the Anugraha of the Siddha masters. While receiving its protection and gaining good fortune, one can become truth, become oneself, and achieve samadhi.

From Practicing for Oneself to Practicing for Others

I set out for the secluded parts of the Himalayas in pursuit of extreme samadhi. I was determined, I continued my training, and I achieved samadhi. But even after doing so, my Himalayan journey continued—through Badrinath, Gangotri, Tapoban, Uttarkashi, Keddarnath, Ladakh, Tibet, and Kailas.

I had found truth and surpassed death; I knew everything, through my Himalayan practice. Eventually, satisfied that I had practiced enough, I went from practicing for myself to practicing for others. I began to think that I needed to share the experience of truth with other people. One day I was summoned by Hari Babaji, who told me, "You are a *chittam* (pure soul). Go spread samadhi. Spread the truth and spirituality that transcends the mind. Give diksha and Anugraha. Save people from suffering. Spread peace." I received similar messages from Hari Babaji and other Himalayan sages: "You have achieved samadhi and known truth. Spread love in the world, spread the truth to people so that the world may become peaceful through brotherhood, and the earth and universe achieve oneness."

I was told to awaken people by performing samadhi among them. I was entrusted with the mission of awakening people's inner selves, of giving diksha and saving people. My continued performance of samadhi is the will of the Himalayan Siddha masters.

Demonstrate and Communicate Truth

Samadhi has been performed in public for over five thousand years. However, today it is a dying custom, which is another reason why the Himalayan sages requested that I perform it in public. Performing samadhi in public draws large crowds of people. By connecting with the samadhi Yogi, the heart opens, the ego falls away, and the mind becomes loving.

Since 1991 I have performed samadhi in public every year, in New Delhi, among other places, as well as during the Kumbh Mela, a spiritual festival where many sages gather from across India. The samadhi I perform is the underground samadhi, during which I spend four days in an underground cave that is completely sealed off from the outside world, and where I achieve oneness with the divine. My breathing stops, I transcend death, and become Atman—one with the divine. The four days transcend space and time.

In many Buddhist scriptures, samadhi is spoken of and the importance of enlightenment is explained, but there is ambiguity about whether or not such a thing exists. Through publicly performing samadhi, however, enlightenment and truth can be evidenced, the fact that people are born of the supreme existence—and are, in fact, divine themselves—can be conveyed, and love and peace can be spread.

By the start of 2007, I had performed samadhi in public eighteen times. I was also giving diksha, as well as blessings. Now, through the Anugraha Himalaya Samadhi Program, I am making the path to samadhi available, and spreading word of a better life, in which you can be blessed with good fortune and know success. This is my mission. I urge you to wake up, to escape from ignorance!

To Holy Kailas with Pilot Babaji

In Tibet, beyond the Himalayan mountains, is Mount Kailas. It is a holy mountain with a beautiful conical shape, just like Mount Fuji. Mount Kailas is holy to both Hindus and Buddhists. People risk their lives to make the pilgrimage to this over seven-thousand-meter-tall mountain.

Parikrama is the prayer people offer to the mountain by walking around it. It takes about three days to do this, walking from morning until night. Sometimes, very devout Tibetans can be seen performing *wutitoudi* as they pray and walk.

In 1990 and 1995 I went to Mount Kailas, where Hindus say Shiva lives, to offer prayer. In spring 2001, leading a group of Japanese people, I went again, with Pilot Babaji. From Kathmandu in Nepal, we flew to Lhasa in Tibet, and from there took Land Cruisers to Mount Kailas. We got out at the base and spent three days walking the circumference of the mountain. It was a harsh pilgrimage, but it advanced the purification of mind, body, and soul.

The route to Mount Kailas from India is difficult and very dangerous. In the middle of the journey, you can no longer proceed by bus, and must walk for roughly a month. An Indian spiritual group made the pilgrimage to Mount Kailas at the same time we did, and along the way, four of their members died from altitude sickness. It was tragic, but, in India, to die in a sacred land is regarded as a fortunate thing. Most Indian people, even though they are aware of the risks, have a strong desire to make the pilgrimage to the holy mountain.

Through my training in the Himalayas, I have come to feel truly natural and at ease, and I enjoy life. When I first visited the Himalayas, I was the chairwoman of a cultural center; I still am. At the time, I thought I was perfectly satisfied and happy, but, through my profound training and achievement of samadhi in the Himalayas, I came to experience truth, gain amazing potential, and know true freedom.

Things That Remind Me of the Himalayas

On the Himalayan plateau, the ever-present boulders remain where they are, no matter how strongly the wind blows. If you visit the Himalayas, you can hold that stillness within yourself. You can be as the unmoving boulder in silence.

The Himalayan rivers that make up the tributaries of the Ganges River carry snowmelt unimaginably far downstream. The Indian people, who live in such a hot region, understand the value of this water. The rivers wind here and there, nurturing the fish in the water, and giving moisture to the surrounding plants. They take nothing; they only give, and flow strongly, giving their blessings to the surrounding land.

The sun gives light to all things, continuously; it, too, takes nothing. How different we are, in our acquisitive thirst! We consume and consume and swell up full to bursting. We need to let some of the things inside flow out—let them flow, let them flow! Give, give, and in the end become light. Observing nature can help us understand how to let go of some of the things that are crammed inside, and, in so doing, become free.

The Himalayan wilderness reminds us of what we have lost. And the secret teachings of the Himalayas show us how we can be as free as a bird, as strong as a river, as constant as a rock. By feeling the stillness and joy of the Himalayas, living becomes easier and we begin to grasp the whole.

The stillness and joy of the Himalayas are within the self. Through the Himalayan teachings, you can remove the murkiness that surrounds your body and mind. You can let the sunshine in.

5

The Teachings of the Himalayas: True Yoga

When you hear the word *yoga*, what comes to mind? Perhaps you think of stretching exercises that involve strange poses. This is only a small part of Yoga. In essence, Yoga is the teaching of the collective wisdom of the Himalayan sages, an immortal discipline for realizing the true self. Furthermore, it is a discipline that promotes success and good fortune in life, beautifies body and mind, and also functions as a healing art. Ultimately, it is a science by which to know the truth of life, the universe, and God.

Himalayan Yoga is the quintessential Yoga, the inner Yoga or *antaryatra*. As we have mentioned, the word *yoga* means "union" or "to bind." In the actions of the universe, this action of unity or binding is vital; without such union, our world would not exist. We are the same way; through the union of two, we work in harmony. We walk with two legs; we see with two eyes; we hear with two ears, and we speak with two lips. To love someone requires a second person. The world was created by the power of Yoga. We were sent from the font of creation, and, from this place without form, we create union, which takes form and manifests. It then binds with the power of creation and begins to create.

The truth of creation, of nature, is what the Himalayan sages sought and discovered. The sages uncovered this mystery within themselves.

Balance Is a Part of What Yoga Means

The word *yoga* also means "balance": gain balance and proceed toward the true self; gain balance and return to the font. All of creation and action comes from nothingness.

What, then, is within us? Our bodies contain seventy-two thousand *nadi*, or paths, through which energy flows. Among these are 108 important nadi, of which thirteen are of the utmost importance. Of the thirteen, the important are the these three: *pingala*, the solar energy path, which flows along the body's right side; *ida*, the lunar energy, which flows on the left; and *Sushumna*, which flows through the body's center. The left and right energies, pingala and ida, work interchangeably to bring balance, which is what allows us to live. If one or the other becomes too prevalent and balance is disturbed, the condition of the mind and body will worsen.

For example, we tend to think that if something is positive, it is automatically good. However, to use only the positive mind does not bring peace; doing so will unfailingly give birth to a negative mind. Positive and negative must always be maintained in balance; the earth rotates, and we live.

If the "plus" solar energy flowing through the pingala nadi and the "minus" lunar energy flowing through the ida nadi can reach a balance, they melt into one another to form one, and the central nadi, Sushumna, awakens and operates. The holy internal energy, kundalini, flows through the Sushumna nadi. When this energy flows, we can arrive at the gates of the astral body and transcend it to dissolve into the supreme existence.

In this way, the discipline of Yoga carries us to the font of space—nothingness. It brings enlightenment and good fortune, for all.

The Teachings of Yoga and Harmony of Mind and Body

Natural disasters—earthquakes, floods, wildfires, etc.—occur when nature tries to restore balance. Nature is constantly writhing like this as it attempts to harmonize itself. Even the seemingly dormant earth is wriggling, trying to maintain its proper position.

This is also true of our bodies, as each of our bodies is a small universe unto itself. Modern living is full of stressful events such as relationship problems, health problems, work problems, etc. As a result, our energies are extremely turbulent. It is always good to correct the balance of our unbalanced energies, to return that which has become distorted to its original state.

By what, exactly, are our bodies moved? You have probably guessed the answer: our minds. The mind thinks and the body acts accordingly; that is, before the body moves, there is a mind. It follows, therefore, that in order to restore balance to the body, it is necessary to control the mind. The mind, in the first instance, is moved by the life energy, prana, which is born from the font of existence. However, the mind is willful, and once energy is put into it, it automatically goes on its way, and cannot be controlled.

Hence the importance of Yoga, which cleanses the mind and returns it to its original state, stopping all mental processes and ridding it of obtrusive thoughts. Through continued Yoga practice, you will realize that you can use your mind more effectively by making it empty and pure. For example, the Himalayan sages know how to make their bodies like ice, which enables them to live for a long time. They also know how to raise their body temperatures incredibly high, which burns off karma, and how to merge their plus and minus energies to create another-dimensional type of energy. Furthermore, through samadhi, they understand how the universe was made, and how the small universes of our physical bodies came to be how they are.

The Himalayan teachings are a higher-dimensional wisdom, a mystical and sacred treasure that is hardly to be encountered every day. Samadhi Yoga contains the secret teachings of immortality. In the everyday world, only the most elementary, physical level of yoga is taught, as an exercise to move the body, which may help improve health and beauty. It has become a fad. The meditation which many people practice now is also only a single part of Yoga. Yoga in essence is the discipline of profound change. In its most advanced form, as Himalayan Yoga, it is a training system that leads to greater health and success in life, helps you become your fundamental self, and become one with God. Through it, you will come to know truth, be at peace, and filled with love and wisdom.

Yoga awakens the inner world and causes it to evolve. Through sustained Yoga practice, not only will you gain knowledge and increase your power of concentration, but you will also truly experience and understand your body, mind, and true self.

The First Step of Yoga: Yama

Let's move on to the true teachings of Yoga. While many schools of Yoga exist, the most easy-to-understand system is the eight steps of Yoga, which proceed from purification of the body to purification of the mind to purification of the soul. Himalayan Yoga also uses these steps in its purification. The eight steps are: yama, niyama, asana, pranayama, pratyahara, dharana, dhyana, and samadhi. The first two steps, yama and niyama, contain ethical teachings.

Yama means proscription: do not do, speak, or think violent things. All animals are included in its scope. Cherish everything, love without bias, and be honest. Do not steal. Give wisdom, love, and charity to those in need. Also, control your desires: avoid forming unnecessary attachments; don't overindulge in food or sex. In sum, the five yama proscriptions are: nonviolence, non-lying, non-stealing, non-expectation of gifts, and non-indulgence of the senses.

We all, on occasion, feel dislike. We also feel upset or angry with things we don't like. In such cases, try to think the opposite: regain balance, reflect on the self, and, by forgiving people, control your heart. The proscriptions of yama may seem obvious but think about it: if we all succeeded at these obvious things, then surely our newspapers wouldn't be filled with stories of violence every day.

Many of us like to think that our minds are relatively pure and that it's not in our nature to do bad things. But, in today's competitive society, is this really true? If a colleague has something good happen to them, don't we get jealous or envious, perhaps even a little depressed? If someone has power over us, we tend not to respect their position, and develop a negative mindset toward them. It is all too easy to become progressively more negative. In such a state of confusion, it is impossible to awaken ourselves, and so much easier to reflexively reject others.

Please don't take the proscriptions of yama at face value. Examine them deeply, take their lessons to heart, and act on them as chances to grow.

Purification: The Second Step, Niyama

The second step is called *niyama*, observance; it promotes the doing of good deeds. If one does good things to purify the mind and body, without forming attachments, it will lead to the liberation of the soul and the true self. This is the doing of good deeds in order to purify karma; it is for the betterment of society and involves the nurturing of love and the increasing of good energy. It is good karma for the salvation of the soul.

The first step of niyama is cleanliness, in the name of purity. To keep the body clean, Yogis will clean their outsides with water, and sometimes paint themselves with mud as purification. They will also meticulously clean the inside of their bodies. There are some who will clean their stomachs and noses, and even down to their intestines.

The Indian people bathe in the holy Ganges River to remove impurities from their minds and bodies. The way we bathe, too, is an action that is linked to preventing egoism. There are many among the Brahman, the Indian equivalent of monks, who do not eat that which others have made, but only what they have made themselves. This too is a way of keeping with niyama. It is important to maintain the cleanliness of the body by eating only that which is natural, with little or no additives (which place undue stress on the body).

The next question is: How do you purify the mind? A good place to start is to only use kind and beautiful words with your partner, and never to speak ill of them. Use words that are filled with feelings of gratitude and compliment your partner often. It is important to do this, just as it is important to speak with love. People often use words indicative of a dissatisfied or blaming mind—even parents use such words with their children. If we cannot fix this human problem, we will not have good fortune.

Clearly, then, the first teachings of Yoga are decidedly moral in tone. This is because, if we are to reach the ultimate goal of life—enlightenment—and achieve greater success, the mind and body must be purified, must be at peace. If you are to reach this goal, you must actively nurture good energy in your daily life. Without purification of the mind and body, there is no succeeding on this path. Yama and niyama are crucial first steps.

The Meaning Behind Asceticism and Reciting Mantras

In the observances of niyama, there is more than a trace of asceticism. But please be assured: I am not asking you to do difficult things. The core of niyama is comprised of things that anyone can do. To keep your silence, or not to speak thoughtlessly, is one way; not to judge others is also a way.

In India, it is common to offer a prayer before one eats and to control the amount one ingests. For example, the practice of half meals, or eating only fruits for a period of time, helps to purify the body and mind, and increases a person's ability to withstand pain, heat, or cold.

Listen to the stories of those who have knowledge of truth and intone the holy words of mantras and sutras. By chanting a mantra, the heart is made pure, and karma is cleansed. Holy sound waves are things to be ridden; when they spread within you, you will become closer to your true self and God.

The most important thing is faith; it is the keystone to becoming your true self and meeting God. Gratitude and belief in the invisible existence that supports the mind and body is indispensable. Believe in the self and believe in God. Believe, also, in the master who leads you to enlightenment. The essence of these three beliefs is the same. This is where you surrender and offer up everything. Then, you receive protection and blessings, you gain the power to live, and become able to evolve and further refine the self.

Through yama and niyama, you can purify your mind and body and strengthen your willpower. These steps are essential if you are to advance to the next step, and if your soul is to attain its glow.

Testimonial: The Nation's Top Year-on-Year Sales
from a store manager in Kanagawa

My mind was constantly fragmented, and I felt uneasy about many things—myself, my job, my relationships, etc. However, I met Yogmata, and she taught me how to meditate. By practicing every day, I was able to change.

I work at a chain store that has over ten stores nationwide. Last year saw good results in sales, so the company president asked me if I would take over as the store manager at the most problematic store we had. This store was wretched. The staff were self-centered, unfocused, and disobedient. In addition, there were many dissatisfied customers with multiple complaints, and too few staff, which made overtime an everyday occurrence. No store manager lasted long there. Any time before, I would have refused such a hard position, but there was a part of me that strangely accepted the idea as something necessary.

Such was my workplace, but the things I considered problems gradually began to resolve themselves thanks to my continued meditation and faith that Yogmata was watching over me. The staff's rebellious attitude disappeared, as did those customers with lots of complaints, and on top of that, somewhere along the line our year-on-year sales growth became the top in the nation. All this happened even though I didn't especially apply my willpower to raising sales. Even now, late-night overtime is common, and we are still in a state of almost no days off, but I haven't collapsed and have been able to continue working.

Our customers who came to return faulty merchandise would leave with a word of thanks; if they left something with us and it was damaged, in the end we were able to see them off looking satisfied. The other staff also ceased causing huge commotions over little things.

In this way, no matter what happened, I was able to keep my chin up and move forward. My mood improved, my personal relationships improved, my progress at work went up, and I began to receive high evaluations.

The Third Step of Yoga: Asana

The third step of Yoga is the balancing of the body. It is called *asana* and refers to the physical Yoga postures. A long time ago, around the time Buddha was still living, the physical aspects of Yoga were not particularly developed, and it was more of an inner science. Today, physical yoga is common, and this in itself can be taken as proof of how distorted our bodies and minds have become.

Thousands of yoga postures have been developed over the years, but there are still eighty-four basic poses. These include the lotus posture, half lotus posture, accomplished posture, and pleasant posture. They are all postures for meditation that stabilize the body's energy and unify the spirit.

The goal of these poses is to put the body in order. If the body is warped, then energy will flow in the direction of that warp. We internalize our daily stresses and our bodies become a confused mess; we also use our minds inefficiently, which causes energy-related stress and creates confusion.

Those who do brainwork only use their heads; those who eat too much overuse their internal organs. Those who drink too much alcohol put great stress on their liver. Those who play golf twist their bodies unnaturally—there is no shortage of ways in which the body can be used unevenly.

If we perform the same actions in our work and lifestyles, hold the same postures, or our bodies are used unevenly by our mind's karma, then our energies will not flow uniformly and our bodies will become uneven, possessed of unhealthy habits. If the unevenness goes unaddressed, it becomes the root of instability or disease. It is necessary, then, to disentangle the body through various actions.

The asanas of yoga take most of their hints from the movements of animals. The naturalness that animals possess is reflected in these figures; by moving like them, people can regain their lost natural power.

To Be Able to Naturally Solve Many Problems

In the United States, asana yoga is experiencing a huge boom in popularity. It is a yoga brought over from India, but people easily become entrapped by its eccentricity, and its essential teachings are difficult, so its essential truth is often not conveyed.

As a health practice, yoga exercises unwind the body, which then unwinds the mind; joints become looser and the functioning of one's internal organs improves. The movements are slow and can be performed at your own pace. However, only following this one part of yoga will cause you to form an attachment to your body—it will not lead you to samadhi. If you continue in such a vein, you will succeed merely in developing your ego, not your mind's true perception. The disciplines of the mind and body have to be practiced together.

To make the body flexible, it is important to think about the level that is right for you and what you want to achieve, and to be both realistic about and familiar with your current mental and physical states.

The wisdom of Yoga is not to aim to perform physical exercises well or to win against others. The goal is to create a mind and a body that can resolve any problems that might arise in a natural way. By purifying the mind and body, the truth becomes clear and perception deepens. If your attachment to your body disappears, your body will become healthier, and you will be able to manifest your abilities at their highest level.

Working from the ground up causes solutions to problems to arise naturally. Furthermore, if you possess the grace of the Himalayan Anugraha, then deep wisdom will come forth. Your mind and body will be balanced and cleansed, and you will be led to resolution from the invisible place deep within.

The Meaning of the Tree Pose

We all have various desires, and our minds and bodies move around, this way and that. Often, when we are still, our minds start to play games. When the body is moving, blood is directed to it and consciousness is focused on it: so, the head stays comparatively clear. However, if the body is unused, the mind begins to imagine, and it starts to play. If you carefully watch your mind while continuing to hold a single pose, the internal monologue will eventually quieten down. One of the forms used for this is the tree pose, or vriksasana.

Some trees live for hundreds, even thousands, of years. The Jomon Sugi tree on Yakushima is said to be seventy--two hundred years old, a divine, old tree. Vriksasana is a pose to unify the spirit by continuously standing in the manner of a tree. It has the effect of calming the mind, balancing the body, and nurturing the power of a unified spirit, and is one of the basic yoga poses.

Some Indian practitioners have stood continuously for decades. One such practitioner that I saw was very extreme and stood on one leg without ever switching. As a result, his other leg seemed about to rot, but his mind was like heaven. Such practitioners have crossed a certain line and are no longer trapped by the body. There was also a practitioner who continuously stood in the Ganges River. He was never swept away or knocked over in his journey to attain a steadfast mind.

Tree Pose

Stand up perfectly straight on one leg as if you were a tree.

Bend the left leg at the pelvis and raise it, take the instep in both hands, place it in the groin of the right leg and open the pelvis.

Lower the shoulders, drop the chin, and put the palms of the hands together in front of the breast.

Being careful not to lose balance, hold this position for twenty to sixty seconds.

When done, switch legs and repeat.

Do not aim somewhere or move around here and
there but stand still and make the mind tranquil.
By learning the concept of "I am here," the bigger
picture spontaneously comes into view.

Asana Is Moving Meditation

No matter how much you succeed in life, if working too
hard causes your body to fall apart, it is meaningless. Nevertheless, if you simply jog or go to a fitness club without
thinking, the exercise will only produce a superficial effect.
If you truly want to do something effective for your body,
you must exercise while being aware of your present self.

Similarly, in the yoga asana, it is necessary to perceive
the motions. Simply doing the asana will get the blood
flowing and support your health, but that doesn't mean
it's good to do them in a stiff manner.

Throw away the ego. Practice with a view to becoming
empty and try to move with your perception. Understand
what's within you, so you can harmonize body and mind.

Order the Breath, Cleanse the Body and Mind: Step Four, Pranayama

The fourth step is the order and control of breath. If one's
breathing becomes disordered, the mind does likewise, so
one can cleanse the mind and body by ordering the breath.
In addition, breath brings oxygen into the body, which in
turn promotes metabolism, thus cleansing the body.

This next step of yoga is called *pranayama* because it
uses breath to regulate the life energy of prana. Breathing can be a conscious action, even if we usually breathe
unconsciously. Disorder of the mind becomes disorder of
the breath, so your breath can give good insight into your

inner state. Think of the breath as a bridge between your internal and external selves.

The movements of the life energy, prana, are finely divided into five types, each with its own name: vidana, the energy that raises things up; prana, which takes in life; samana, the power to burn and change; apana, which lowers energy; and vyana, which moves the whole body. By purifying, strengthening, and controlling each prana, the internal self is awakened and purified, and truth becomes knowable.

In this way, pranayama, which means to regulate prana, is the control of energy; also, since breath exists as an entrance, it is a breathing method. Because the flow of energy immediately affects the mind, not to mention that the breath flows into the autonomic nervous system, this breathing method has the potential to cause injury. It must be used with care. The best course, as always, is to be taught by a master.

A Mind That Sees Without Getting Trapped: Step Five, Pratyahara

The fifth stage is *pratyahara*. This stage is about restraining and controlling the senses to prevent the entrapment of the mind. It strongly resembles the saying, "See no evil. Hear no evil. Speak no evil." Pratyahara cleanses the senses and strives to preserve a steadfast and peaceful mind.

Incidentally, the three truths or three virtues embodied by the famous Three Monkey Carvings of Mizaru, Kikazaru, and Iwazaru, or See-No-Evil, Hear-No-Evil, and Speak-No-Evil, that are engraved on the front wall of the sacred horse stables at Nikko Toshogu Shrine are said to have come to Japan through the teachings of Tendai Buddhists.

We all have five sense organs: eyes, ears, nose, tongue, and skin. It is necessary to better them. We have two eyes, two ears, and our noses have two nostrils. In this way, each one is balanced, which allows it to function properly. Deep within the eye is vision. Deep within the ear is hearing. On the tongue is taste, in the nose is smell, and on the skin is the sense of touch. All must be cleansed, if they are to work properly.

We all know sensitive people who feel things too strongly, as well as those at the stoical end of things, who struggle to feel anything at all. Rather than becoming such a person, it is necessary to reach a balance. Cleanse and control your senses to make them unswayable.

We are often picky about the things we encounter through our senses. What controls their workings, exactly? Once again, it is the mind. We are all familiar with how this works: "I want to see!" "I don't want to hear it!" This is the mind controlling the senses.

How much better it is to cleanse the mind so you can experience things as they are. If the mind can become free of obstructive thoughts, it will not be swayed. If the mind is swayed, it immediately thinks: this is scary, that is beautiful, I want more of this, I want less of that. The senses respond to the mind and work.

If you can control your breath and energy, you will be able to control your mind. By breathing properly, both the body and mind are cleansed. If you breathe with a greedy mind, a twisted sort of energy will develop, and balance will be lost—this is a very common occurrence.

I am not suggesting you should breathe a lot. Just as medicine ceases to work as you take more of it and build up a tolerance, so breath too will cease to work as your excitement grows stronger and titillates the ego. The breathing method is an exercise in mental concentration, but it can be an exercise in developing awareness as well if the breath is examined closely. In this way, we can come to understand our state of mind.

For example, when we are mad, we breathe violently. When you are full of angry feelings and feel ready to spit hurtful words, it is important to take a deep breath, and breathe calmly. In doing so, the mind will become tranquil.

In this way, through breathing, it is possible to control the mind. By consciously practicing peaceful breathing, it is possible to have a peaceful heart.

Cleansing of the Senses and Cleansing of the Mind

The fact that Yogis are able to live in the Himalayas is due to no other cause than their knowledge of how to control their minds and bodies. For example, the energy of the right side of the body, pingala, works to warm the body, so by controlling that it becomes possible to live in a very cold place.

Conversely, in order to preserve the human body for a long time, one can control the energy of the left side of the body, ida. By cooling the body, its cells metabolize much more slowly. That is why meat and vegetables put in the refrigerator last longer. However, if one becomes too cold, then it becomes harder to control the mind.

Pingala is solar energy, while ida is lunar energy. Also, as we have mentioned, there is Sushumna in the body's center. Sometimes the energy in pingala is working, and at other times the energy in ida is working; they are external energies, and through them, life works in positive or negative ways.

Having once reached the advanced stage of controlling one's senses in pratyahara, even if the eyes are open and can see, the mind is unmoved. This is a freer, unwavering condition. Through pratyahara, one chooses to have the mind un-swayed by what is seen or heard and chooses only good words.

Many people only see external things as being bad; they choose bad things and have a tendency to think pessimistically. In order to not become like that, it is important to cleanse the mind itself. If you can cleanse the senses that are connected with the mind's workings, and control the senses, you will truly develop the mind's awareness

Gaining True Freedom by Cleansing the Senses

A cleansed mind does not judge; it enjoys a peaceful state. Also, when we are working hard at something, the mind is focused and stable. However, most of us have wavering minds. At such a level, it is all too easy to select worrying or stressing, or another negative option. It is necessary to return to your center, where your mind is unobstructed, at those times when you are prone to worry or stress.

One of the first steps of Yoga, the faith of niyama, is very important here. By believing in a pure existence, you can connect with the center of the universe. But you have to believe in yourself.

Our sense organs are high-functioning antennae. Think of the times you've found yourself in a room full of people you don't know—doesn't your eye, somehow, pick out the one person you do know? This is because we don't see with our eyes only, but also with our minds. What we attract—think of a compass, or a magnet—differs, depending on the kind of person we are, and our karma. If we can rid ourselves of our karma, we won't be swayed, no matter what comes our way. This is the path to true freedom.

Normally, we use our sense antennae to understand the outside world. By closing off the senses and relieving the mind of its work, it becomes possible to look at the inner reality and see how it works. It is good to rest the sense organs so that, for a time, we are not swayed by our senses and can enter our inner selves. In doing so, it becomes easier to concentrate and one can unite the spirit.

A useful exercise is to choose a single thing, use a single sense, and cleanse that sense. In doing so, one can properly take in that one thing, and, without being swayed by the other senses, focus naturally.

Becoming One with the Holy Energy

Not seeing while truly understanding is completely different from not seeing without understanding. Those who don't believe in anything in the world and want to see nothing have probably closed their mind's eye at some point. However, in so doing, they have closed off all available avenues for their active energy and fallen into an inert state. To not see while truly understanding is totally different. Everything becomes clear and the energies are working at their highest level, unless they are unnecessary, in which case they lie dormant.

The mind always has two natures, good and bad. If the mind is always good, it will tire; the same is true of the bad—both consume energy. If you can take comfort in not using the mind while cleansing the bad mind and becoming one with holy energy, you can recharge your energy and use it productively.

A great deal of our energy is eaten up by stress, even when we are sitting down or sleeping. We worry about this and that and our energy flows automatically. We wake up exhausted even though we have slept well. Even if we clean out the mind, it immediately stagnates. To recharge that energy, try to "see no evil"—in other words, while understanding and watching, try not to be swayed, but stay focused on simply watching.

Look with a pure mind and continue to cleanse it. By looking from your true self, the object can be detached. This is a practice of high-level perception, as performed by samadhi masters. If you are able to come this far, don't stop at pratyahara; connect with even higher-level meditation practices on your way to enlightenment.

Gain Power Through Spiritual Unity: Step Six, Dharana

Dharana translates as "concentration" in English, or *gyonen* in Japanese; it is concerned with uniting the spirit. The power of spiritual unity is indispensable for improving social life.

Depending on the object of our spiritual unifying, we can gain a variety of powers. If you focus on something pure that unifies the spirit, the mind can rest. Your focus will then expand and become a meditation.

The Indian people are used to focusing on God or a master and receiving power from one of them. From a young age, they practice focusing on statues that reflect the powers of the gods of the universe. To think on that with love is concentration, a faith known as *bhakti*. In bhakti one believes in the Hindu gods, such as Shiva or Vishnu, or an enlightened master. Tibetan Buddhists believe in the Buddha or their leader, the Dalai Lama. A believing mind has the power to accept; it is unwavering and successful.

The Indian people show gratitude for things that displease them, accepting them as a lesson. They greet people who displease them with reverence, their hands folded in prayer—again, because they believe the gods have sent the disagreeable person, as part of a lesson. There is a sense of reliance, as if everything is at God's discretion. Through Yogic concentration, we can understand and gain this power.

If you perform dharana, you will be able to realize your dreams through faith. If you don't believe in God, it may be best to focus on objects outside, such as the sea, the sun, the moon, or some other natural thing. Other methods of dharana involve focusing on the body's energy center, or on thought.

Regardless of whether or not you believe, everything is allowed to live by the power of God, and, at the deepest level, all created things are divine. Concentration draws out this power and strengthens it, settling the tumults of the mind.

Step Seven, Meditation and Dhyana; and Step Eight, Samadhi

The seventh step of Yoga is *dhyana*, which means meditation. If you have reached this level and can unify the spirit and become the essence of everything, you can let go of everything and be free. Eventually you will be totally free, unswayed by anything. Within this stage is a state of being free of all ties and obstructive thoughts. Dhyana is transliterated in Chinese as Zen'na—the origin of Zen.

The secret technique of Himalayan Yoga samadhi is a meditation on sound which dissolves worldly desires and produces a deep stillness. Another technique of Himalayan Yoga is kriya meditation, a meditation on light that smoothly cleanses karma, leads to a deep meditation, and causes change. Both of these meditation techniques can help you become an aware, creative, successful person.

And so we come to the eighth and last stage of yoga, *samadhi*. Though it is treated as a single stage, samadhi has different stages or kinds. In Siddhi or psychic samadhi, you unite with the subject of meditation, and become it. In samprajnata samadhi, or concentration according to seed, you unite with thought. Lastly, there is asamprajnata samadhi, or concentration with no seed, which is the true and final stage of samadhi. This involves transcending all earthly desires and becoming your true self. That is, you completely surpass your body and mind, arrive at your Atman, and become free. From here, you become divine, an ultimate existence or super-consciousness. Then, you become nothingness, free from thought, or moksha. You have achieved total enlightenment.

To Become the True Self

High-level, true samadhi is the only path to enlightenment for becoming truth, knowing the true self, and becoming Atman. If you become truth—that is, you become the soul itself, you become an existence called *Atman* in Sanskrit. Atman is also called shinga, being, existence, or self.

To go beyond this is to become Paramatman—the higher self, a divine consciousness. Beyond this, one becomes the supreme self, Brahman, the super-consciousness or supreme existence.

Samadhi is the path to true enlightenment. To attain it, you must first enter yourself and realize exactly who you are. By perceiving the body, mind, and Buddha nature individually, by experiencing them, you will become enlightened. Then, by transcending each, you will arrive at the truth. Be going step by step through Anugraha diksha, by learning the meditation techniques for each step, by honing and refining your temperament and bodily traits, and by exercising your mind and body, you can smoothly proceed on the path to enlightenment. Remember that Anugraha is the grace of God; it can only be performed by someone who has achieved samadhi.

Unpublicized Himalayan Yoga

The eighth step of Yoga brings knowledge of the truth, causes significant inner change, creates inner beauty, and is the path to enlightenment. This path—created by Siddha and other enlightened masters—has never before been made available to the public.

Since ancient times, a faithful apprentice would first receive the initiation of Anugraha diksha from their master. In doing so, through the shaktipat energy bestowed by the master, the mind, body, and spirit would be fully cleansed and balanced. Today, even in the Himalayas, Yogi who continue this tradition are few. My encounter with these techniques, and attainment of samadhi after embarking on its difficult path, are nothing short of a miracle.

Return to the font of creative energy, know truth, and gain power from the font of creation and life: this is the path to samadhi. Experience in reverse the creative processes of the body, mind, and Buddha nature, and control the prana of everything. That is, return to the pure, original existence, and be enlightened.

Without a master, it is impossible to walk this path and to receive the true blessings of Yoga. However, the chance to learn the secret Himalayan Yoga from a genuine samadhi Yogi is being presented to you, here and now. I see this as my role in life. In order to improve society and the world, and to help people to help each other while becoming better people, I am cleansing people's inner selves, awakening them, and directly connecting them with their true selves.

All wishes are granted when you are on the path to becoming your true self. The lessons of Yoga are not simply health and beauty tips, but a true life science of enlightenment. Himalayan Yoga will enable you to reach your higher self. It will bring harmony, love, and success to your life.

Your Body Is Changeable

The path to samadhi is not to be taken lightly. It is not even accessible without a master. It is, however, possible to know parts of samadhi from something very familiar, which we encounter every day: deep sleep.

During the day, sunlight activates our energy, and we live with vitality. At night, moonlight gently cools us down so we may sleep. While we are asleep, our body and mind recharge. In this way, we live and die each day. Deep sleep is a type of samadhi: we become innocent and touch

God, after which, we are rejuvenated and resurrected. Of course, samadhi itself is not an unknowing sleep; it is like sleeping while being awake.

Himalayan Yoga will enable you to know your body and mind, and to cleanse them. Deep within them lies the soul, and, at the origin beyond everything, is love itself. You can become love itself. You can achieve samadhi and become your true self. Along the way, you will have developed the ability to control your mind and body, gained life energy, and started living a life that is full to the brim with happiness and success.

6

From Religion to That Which Transcends Religion: Himalayan Masters, Gautama Siddhartha, and Jesus Christ

The Mind's Anchor in Painful Times

Throughout history and throughout the world, people have always had religion. All countries have their religions, which give discipline to the lives of their people. Religion teaches humanity and compassion. It promotes mutual understanding and responsibility to society, the nation, and oneself.

When humans feel unsafe, religion blossoms. By believing in the awesome power of an invisible existence, one gains power. Religion protects countries, gives people a sense of security in their lives, and gives them hope that there is a world beyond our own.

Many people seek worldly benefits through worship and prayer. Since ancient times people have revered rocks, mountains, shrines, temples, churches, etc., and built holy shrines and buildings. Ancient sages also valued symbols such as crosses, mandalas, icons, etc., as safe points for the mind.

When the mind gets agitated in everyday life, it finds stability in faith in the divine and in Buddha. All religions have an object of worship like this. Believing in it brings peace of mind and eliminates suffering. The reason people suffer is, to put it bluntly, because they are ignorant. They do not know who they are or what they are doing. Until they know, they will always feel insecure.

However, what if you could connect with something invisible but omniscient, an existence with the wisdom and power to have created everything? Wouldn't the dark clouds roll back? Wouldn't life become easier?

"You Have To" Obsessions in Spiritual Teachings

When I started practicing yoga, I felt uneasy about religion. Certainly, there were those around me who claimed to be studying spirituality and who wholeheartedly preached "Love for all" and "Make this world a heaven." Those who spoke were incredibly generous and kind.

But did their words really issue from a willing love? I felt as though these things were based in a sense of duty, as if people were competing in a race for personal improvement. Some people seemed to be singularly obsessed with "You should do this" or "You should do that."

The pressure bordered on coercion, and the imperative to "be a good person" made everyone tired. It also made people suppress and warp their true emotions and feelings. If one is brimming with vitality and natural love, then naturally one will want to give love. But to work with only the mind toward "Let's be a better person"— well, the ego swells, but the mind spoils.

True good fortune does not lie in grooming one's mind toward perfection; rather, it lies in becoming free of the mind's workings through developing one's own awareness. Even if one has lofty intentions to become a believer in order to become a charitable person by building moral cultivation, the idea is unreasonable unless it is born from within.

If people don't purify their inner selves or proceed toward their true selves, true love will not come to be. Reading about it in a book or getting the idea from someone else is not enough. Faith that is simply an exercise of the mind will only cause the mind to tire.

What Buddha (Sakyamuni) Investigated

Himalayan sages are very familiar with the internal work-ings of the mind. They know how to find tranquility and happiness, and how to avoid being swayed. Buddha learned the lessons of these supreme sages and was able to attain enlightenment.

Buddha—a prince named Gautama Siddhartha—was born around 500 BCE in a small kingdom on the border of India and Nepal called Sakya. He lost his mother seven days after he was born. From the time he was young, Buddha searched within himself, wanting to know why life was so painful, and what the truth was. However, he did not have the freedom to practice, so he continued his scholarly education, married at age sixteen, and became a father of one. By the time he was twenty-nine, he could no longer suppress his desire to know the truth, and he left his castle on a monastic journey.

Since ancient times, Indian society has accepted the practice of going on monastic journeys for those who are seeking enlightenment, or those who want to meet the di-vine. Buddha visited the Himalayan sages in his search for the truth of how to be free of suffering and sickness. Each master had his own way of practicing, and at first Buddha embarked on a practice that was akin to sorcery. It is also said that he was trained in harsh forms of asceticism, in which he would starve himself and abuse his body.

He fumbled at first, but in the end removed the various styles and their embellishments and began a very pure and simple practice. This was the practice of enlightenment, ultimate samadhi. Where he found this practice was Gaya village, later called Buddha Gaya, a place regarded as where the dead are sent to heaven. There, he stopped un-der a Bodhi tree and made up his mind to sit unmoving, no matter what, until he found truth. Through medita-tion, he found enlightenment and became his true self.

This was the winter of Buddha's thirty-fifth year, before dawn on December eighth. He attained enlightenment—we call this "completing the path"—and returned. He explained to the people, "Causes are formed by the mind, and through fate are materialized into effects. Life revolves within that fate, that karma. Thus, if one has a good mind, good things will come."

He taught affection and compassion, as well as the importance of the mind that is unwavering and free of obstructive thoughts. He taught that this world is an illusion created by our minds, and that, if we look deep within our minds, we will find that there is nothing. He conveyed the importance of people living as affection itself. These lessons formed the many sutras that have been passed down to us today.

Meditation to Samadhi—Christ's Case

Five hundred years after Buddha, in the town of Nazareth in Galilee, Jesus Christ began to spread the words of love, wisdom, and service to men: "Love your enemies, do good to those who hate you" (Luke 6:27). It is said that Christ meditated in the wasteland for forty days. I heard there was historical evidence of the place where Christ practiced in north India. I have been to that temple in Ladakh.

The eminent soul known as Christ devotedly walked the path of truth, became aware of the truth, and preached true happiness. In the gospel according to Matthew, Christ says, "Blessed are the poor in spirit, for theirs is the kingdom of heaven" (Matthew 5:3). The word *poor* is easy to misconstrue, but I am confident that, if you have read this far, you understand Christ's meaning, and that he was speaking of "humble people who has discarded arrogance, fetters, ostentatiousness, and other desires."

It is said that, after three years of proselytizing, Jesus rose from the dead three days after being hanged on the cross, at age thirty-three, on the outskirts of Jerusalem. I believe that his death and rebirth is without doubt a demonstration of samadhi. By saving everybody through performing this miracle of resurrection, his teachings spread throughout the world.

It can be said, then, that Buddhism, Hinduism, and Christianity were born from the teachings of the Himalayan sages.

What Religious Faith Brings About

The teachings of Buddha and Christ live on today and are still widely read in the Bible and the sutras. The power of people's belief, of their faith, is a powerful force. This is evident in the fantastic buildings, temples, and churches people have built.

However, it is also sadly true that religion has been the seed for war and conflict across the world since ancient times. Though their fundamental goals and eventual destinations are the same, believers are caught up in particulars with each side convinced that their teachings are the "best." It is very unfortunate that the pursuit of purity should give birth to conflict. Sometimes the sole purpose of the conflict is to strengthen or grow a particular faction or organization.

All religions advocate moral teachings while receiving power from faith. In society, it is important to respect one another, be considerate, and continuously improve people's lifestyles. On the other hand, people tend to think that dogma is absolute; they believe in the words and try to live as they say. While this can strengthen the mind, it can also cause people to get overly hung up on the words they are trying to follow. This causes the ego to swell, from too many thoughts of "I know," and makes people resistant to accepting anything that strikes them as "other."

To attain true good fortune, the mind must be free. Try not to understand things with your head only but strive to know the truth and evolve your consciousness. Enter the self, purify the mind, and change from within. Know and free the mind and body, then transcend them to know the true self, and go on to become one with the divine. I am asking a lot, but the path that was previously unavailable to you can now, through Himalayan Yoga, be made clear.

All religions contain teachings that explain the sacredness of faith and help spread knowledge of the importance of gratitude. Many people take these good lessons to heart, strengthen their minds, and are saved. The development of the mind is directly linked to the proper functioning in the society and it is now possible to walk on the path leading to personal transformation of the highest quality. Nevertheless, in order to progress along the path of truth, you must open your heart, connect with your true self and the divine, and be free of all that imprisons you.

It is crucial to awaken the self. Believe in yourself. Believe in your karma. Become an enlightened person. Have full knowledge of the universe within, and reform yourself from within. Grasp absolute happiness instead of mere happiness of mind. Experience real truth and become enlightened. Transcend your mind and body and become the master of yourself.

Yes, this path is difficult, and those who have been given the chance to walk it are few in number. Even for some of those who have been given the chance, lifetimes of practice have been required. This path is of the purest, highest-level teaching. It is the path sought by the ancient scholars; the path that leads to true self-realization; the path that gave birth to all religions. It is the original teaching.

The path to enlightenment is the highest goal for all of the world's religions. The way to truly attain it is through Himalayan Yoga.

Himalayan Yoga has been passed down orally from master to apprentice since the first Himalayan sages encountered truth over five thousand years ago. However, this tradition is fading, and the true samadhi Yogi are few in number, even in the Himalayas, and they do not visit the world below. Yes, there are many people who call themselves master or guru; sadly, almost none of them have found the real truth.

Even if you devoted your life to scouring the Himalayas, it would be impossible to find a single samadhi Yogi. Even if you somehow succeeded, to receive a blessing from such a Yogi would be meaningless, if your karma wasn't in order.

In India there are many who call themselves Hindu practitioners, but most of them don't pursue enlightenment. The moment they begin their ascetic journey, many fetters are removed, and their life becomes more comfortable. They enjoy the freedom of the practitioner's life, but few of them ever achieve enlightenment.

Long ago in India, only the king, nobility, Brahman, or other intelligentsia wished for enlightenment. The general public respected and believed in the divine while seeking blessings for a better life, but they didn't pursue personal enlightenment. Buddha was a prince, and Pilot Babaji comes from noble stock. The enlightened path of truth-seeking is the path they chose to walk. The general public worships at a shrine or temple, or simply bathes in the Ganges. Those who have performed samadhi training, who have experienced the divine beyond their minds and bodies, are rare indeed.

I have succeeded in bringing Himalayan Yoga to Japan, but this isn't enough. Global warming is progressing, and the environment is deteriorating; the earth's ecosystems are in disarray. To prevent further worsening of our situation, many people must be purified through Himalayan Yoga, become meditators who bring about great abundance in nature, and become enlightened individuals.

Even if you fail to reach an enlightened state of mind, by envisioning it and by practicing, I truly believe the earth can be saved, and, in the process, you can be healed and go on to lead a life of abundance, within and without.

Meeting the Right Master Is Important

I have said that it is all but impossible to meet a sage who knows the truth, and that only a true guru or samadhi Yogi who has achieved samadhi can guide you on the path to enlightenment. If you err in choosing a guide, the consequences can be severe, so I urge you to be careful.

If you travel to India, you will meet a variety of practitioners. At the Kumbh Mela festival many such sages gather under one roof. Kumbh Mela is a giant, month-long spiritual event held once every twelve years and hosted at one of the four great holy sites, Haridwar, Allahabad, Nashik, or Ujjain. The last one was held in 2007 in Allahabad. Along with many sages and worshipers, the general public participates in a river bathing. Each guru has a temporary practice area set up—in fact, there are so many genuine masters whom one may follow that nobody knows.

One guru says to balance a pot of fire on your head; another says to paint your body in ashes. There are always some hippie-like Westerners who, upon hearing this, immediately apprentice themselves in this way.

Returning to the True Self Is the Truth Indeed

In India there are those who claim to be reincarnations of gods. Whether or not they truly are is unclear, but they claim to be incarnations of Vishnu, Buddha, Maitreya, etc. There are also those who say they are reincarnations of Christ or other great sages of the past. A person cannot truly become a god; a god is a different type of entity. To say that you are the reincarnation of such-and-such a god is simply the work of the mind.

It is possible, however, to reach self-realization and become an offshoot of the divine. Truth, then, is not the mind becoming a god, but returning to the font of one's own existence, to the true self, which is where to locate God. That is, the enlightenment of the divine comes within the self through the purifying of the self. This is what it means to truly become the font of all existence. It is most definitely not an assumption of the mind.

The Indian people wish to meet the divine and receive its blessing. This does not mean that the practitioners who gather at Kumbh Mela are practicing to return to the essential self or to transcend death. At Kumbh Mela I met a practitioner, a sadhu, who spent decades standing by a river on one leg like a crane. Even to the point of causing great imbalance in his body, he was not swayed; he continued in his belief in the divine and fell into that state completely.

One practitioner I met in the interior sacred land of Badrinath had spent twenty years holding up his right hand. His right arm was as thin as a tree branch, and his fingernails were tens of centimeters long. Constantly holding up an arm gives birth to thoughts of lowering that arm. When that mind disappears, it has been transcended and significant change occurs. No doubt this practitioner had difficulty dressing and undressing, but he had learned this method from a guru, and his pure, angelic smile left a strong impression.

Suffice to say that, depending on the kind of master you encounter, the method of practice can vary dramatically. Some practitioners go for years without eating; others sleep on mountains of needles. There are even powerful practitioners who pull trucks with thin ropes attached to their teeth.

There are also sadhu who do Yoga, but in India those who practice the essence of Yoga and those who perform samadhi are given the honorific title of Yogi.

The Existence That Guides from Darkness to Light

As stated previously, the *gu* of *guru* means darkness, and the *ru* means light. A guru, then, is an entity that guides you from darkness to light.

All people are born from light. However, because they have minds, the light becomes clouded. It gets clouded when the mind works too much. Once that happens, a guru is needed to guide you back onto the true path.

What kind of guide should you follow and practice under? A samadhi Yogi—that is, a guru who has experienced real samadhi. I ask you to meet with such a guru and connect with the truth. You will transcend everything and become one who knows all.

The practice of truly changing from within is part of the secret teachings of the Himalayas and the true life science of Yoga: purify the body, mind, and soul, change into subtle waves, and reach the level of essence. These are the secret lessons of transcending the mind, body, and even the soul. They are the secret techniques that have been gathered together by Himalayan sages over millennia.

In India, there is a great variety of masters with many styles of teaching. For example, the masters of the bhakti Yoga tradition say to aim for enlightenment through faith in the divine and love. Bhakti Yoga, at its basic level, does not involve the body very much. It sees everything as something given by the divine; even disease is received as a present from God and is regarded as good fortune.

There are also masters who actively participate in song and dance. Among masters who sing the devotional songs known as *bhajan* there are those who gather many followers and have large temples. Certainly the Indian people like to sit for long periods listening to melodious songs about myths and legends. Their love of God is strong. There are also masters of hatha Yoga, which reveres the breath and movement of the body. Clearly, there are numerous spiritual paths.

Himalayan Yoga, including the eight steps, is the direct teaching of the power of wisdom from a Siddha master samadhi Yogi. It makes life simpler, invites success, and shows the path toward true enlightenment. With an Anugraha blessing straight from a samadhi Yogi, you can safely and comfortably evolve and witness miracles being born.

Basics of Safe Practice and Yoga

In its essence, Yoga is a practice that purifies karma, and leads to beauty in inner essence, mind, and body; it is a path to enlightenment through transcendent change. Even if you start to practice Yoga because you are dieting, it remains connected with intrinsically polishing your inner self, so there is a very good chance that your initial reason will come to change. Yoga works in deep places to evolve your consciousness; your mind will become more beautiful as it becomes comfortable with itself.

Incidentally, the well-known pioneers who sought to spread Yoga throughout the world were Swami Vivekananda (1863–1902) and Paramahansa Yogananda (1893–1952). They preached Yoga in a Christian arrangement throughout the United States and Europe. They lived in the United States and made Yoga commonplace. It is said that Vivekananda had a huge effect on Tenshin Okakura.

On the path to inner beauty, the first and most important step is the initiation of diksha. This initiation is for the transmission of energy known as shaktipat, which is samadhi power given by a master, as well as instruction of secret techniques. The diksha of Himalayan Yoga is a secret, powerful ceremony that other gurus cannot perform. It purifies your karma directly, opens the door to your font of existence, and awakens you.

There are many types of diksha, such as fundamental diksha (guru diksha), mantra diksha, aspas diksha, shaktipat diksha, kriya diksha, kripa diksha, sanskara diksha, healing diksha, Anugraha diksha, and samadhi diksha, as well as advanced diksha. Through these, you are initiated and purified, after which, you can evolve and change quickly.

In the ceremony of fundamental diksha, you will be instructed in the secret meditation technique, and your master will give you a mantra. Then you become an apprentice and connect with your master. The sound waves of the mantra safely and effectively purify your mind as well as protect you. There are many types of sacred waves that are used for different purposes. Each is taught and can be advanced depending on the nature and level of the practitioner.

These sacred waves of sound are precious. They hold the power of the divine and, while protecting a person as their lifetime guardian force, they purify the mind. The waves of sound can be thought of as sound before it has become words.

All waves of sound are born of the sun and space. They are born when a ray of sunlight strikes empty space. That vibration transforms into sacred waves. A similar system exists within the body: the light and sound energies within the body form the source of sound (sound of seed), and when that resonates with the waves of a mantra, the mind is purified.

The Most Important Waves of the Source

Within the waves is the sound of the root of the universe, the root sound of everything. It consists of pure energy, active energy, and dark energy. These three energies are called sattva, rajas, and tamas. Sacred waves come from these three dimensions. They are the source of all words and the root sounds of all understanding. They can be thought of as the sounds of the supreme existence.

These three energies—pure, active, and dark—are the energies of the neutron, positron, and electron. Each of them activates and purifies different part. All energies have its own root power, own center, which is equivalent to individual God(s). There is male energy, female energy, and the two in combination, as well as the energies of wisdom, plenty, action, nirvana, creation, power, healing, ability, etc. Each is the energy of Gods.

Samadhi masters are profoundly familiar with the properties of these energies and know the techniques to activate them. Their power reaches into space as well as the root of the body and causes transformations in various dimensions. Only a true master understands what waves match what person, how that person should practice, and how they should meditate. Masters give power to these waves and that power works through them.

Be Purified by Sacred Waves

The sacred waves of sound are the divine. They are the sounds of the root of existence. By taking those energies and channeling them, focusing them, and, with awareness, spreading them, your karma will be purified along with your mind and body. The basis of thought is sound, and through the sacred waves of your mantra, your thoughts are purified, and you can separate yourself from them.

Separated thoughts that have lost their destinations may start to reel. If so, they should return to their respective origins and disappear through the power of the sacred sounds and your own watchfulness. Let's take anger as an example. If you and your anger are one, you are so bound up in it that you don't know what's what. However, if you notice, "Ah, I'm angry," and focus your consciousness on the sacred waves, you will be purified by the power of the root sound.

In this way, the sacred wave method of meditation works to purify the body while purifying the inner mind and enabling change. If you continue this method of meditation for a long period of time, your inherent qualities will rise and blossom, and eventually the sacred waves may penetrate down even as far as the genetic level and recompose you.

The exercises of yoga improve blood flow. However, simply doing the poses does not purify the mind. In order to further the mind's awareness and to bring about change within, these root waves function strongly to create good energy.

Your mantra is given to you by your master during the purifying ceremony of diksha. Meditation on sacred sound waves is a wonderful practice that protects while safely occasioning profound change. Mantras can be used by anyone from children to the elderly, from the physically strong to the frail. In the end, the sacred sound waves will lead you to samadhi.

Sending Sacred Waves to You

My prayer is for your success.
My prayer is for your family's health.
My prayer is for your family's good fortune.
My prayer is for world peace.
My prayer is for spiritual success.
My prayer is for your true good fortune, your meeting of your true self, and enlightenment.
May the grace of the divine reach you. I am with you.
Life is the most beautiful. Life is the most dynamic.
You have a bountiful and beautiful life.
That is because your life and existence are gifts from the divine.

There is a hidden, mysterious, wondrous world within
you. I am here for you to awaken it, to evolve it. I came
from the Himalayas.
I induct you in diksha and awaken you. I teach you the
Anugraha kriya.
The Anugraha Himalaya Samadhi Program will realize
your true good fortune. It is a scientific method to assur-
edly change you, to create better societies and a better
world.
It makes you succeed in life and makes peace.
Purify thoughts, and all people will have creative, peaceful minds.
Purify your environment, inside and out, and make it
creative.
And so, be healthy, and help your family.
Gain a pure mind, a pure body, and help all. Make the
world peaceful.

Teaching of the Paths of Faith and Love

In the practice of Yoga are the path of love and the path of
faith. In India, in the beginning, there is faith. In addition
to the life of clothing, food, and shelter, there is what can
be called a firmament of faith, which deems all things,
including people, to be products of the power of the invisible existence known as God.

The Indian people live always with God, and so uneas-
iness does not exist. On top of that, they want to meet
the divine in earnest, wish to get closer to a free, powerful
being of love like the divine, and pursue eternal happiness
through practice.

Himalayan Yoga, like Indian yoga, can also be performed by believing in the divine, and then by believing
in a master. Without following a proper guru, trying to
practice meditation or the breathing methods of pranayama can be akin to opening Pandora's box. That is, without

proper guidance, there is the risk that your untamed ego might unite with your increased energy and be amplified as a result. It can be dangerous when energy is tossed about by karma; physiological or psychological imbalance is often the result.

Many people are content simply to love God. In India, for example, there are very fat people who look to be in terrible pain. But, as they believe that God gave them their bodies—and their pain—they are grateful. They accept everything as being the way God wants it to be. All Indian people practice the teachings of love and faith. The austerity of enlightenment, the austerity of Yoga are based on this widespread spiritual foundation creating safe and affirmative environment for the practice.

Testimonial: Receiving Diksha as a Family
from a housewife in Tokyo

It has been just under half a year since I participated in Yogmata's darshan, and three months since all three of us in my family received diksha. Thanks to Yogmata, every day is incomparably more tranquil and happier.

My husband and I as adults feel it, but especially our first-grader son is growing up carefree and engaging himself at his own pace. His teacher at school happily told us how he works hard in school and throws himself into everything with all his might. Admittedly, my son is still a concern, but through connecting with and being loved by Yogmata, I don't worry needlessly; I know my concerns will resolve themselves soon, and I am able to believe and wait.

The time we get to spend together as a family may only be the surprisingly short ten-plus years of his childhood. Since we received diksha, the amount of happiness we can share within that time has gotten stronger and more abundant.

Also, as a couple, we received advanced diksha and my husband was able to participate in a retreat. Since then,

*even our surroundings are filled with good waves. My hus-
band's attitude at home is enriched, and my son looks at
him with such respect and thinks he is so cool. My daily life
has become even more comfortable.*

*While my husband was away at the retreat, even though
I was at home, I felt something pass to me. It was the love
of Yogmata that falls anywhere and everywhere. Certainly
at that time my pathways for receiving grace were opened
wide and I truly felt the light of hope.*

*In our everyday lives, we each meditate and give thanks
that we are connected to and protected by Yogmata. For a
parent or child, it is wonderful to know that, no matter
what, there is a safe place to which we can return, even in
times of unease and worry.*

Thoughts Fly like Arrows

As we have mentioned, Yagya is the equivalent of the Japanese practice of *gomataki*, the burning of cedar incense
in prayer for a blessing. It grants wishes through using a
special mantra while borrowing the power of change from
the energy of fire.

The Yagya performed by a samadhi Yogi has a special effect. By performing it, in addition to the power prayed for
by the samadhi Yogi, your inner power causes change, which
grants your wish and makes it succeed. Yagya is regularly
performed where I live, not just for a person's own wishes,
but also to help realize the wishes of others. It helps many.

It may seem strange, but just about everything you
think of is realized. For this reason, it is vital to think
good thoughts and not bad ones; the thoughts of a purified mind will be realized almost every time.

You may think, "Whatever I think, it won't befoul
me, or anyone else." This is a mistake. If you think, "I
hope that person dies," even for an instant or in jest, the
consequences can be serious. Your thought will fly like
an arrow, and, like an arrow, will pierce that person. If

you think bad things, even as a joke, then you should be prepared for bad things to happen.

Similarly, you mustn't think, "I'm a worthless person." People often complain this way, lightly or even unconsciously. However, if you think negative things, they will inevitably come true, and certainly cause you trouble—if not in this life, in the next.

Regardless of whether or not we are meditators, regardless of however pure or impure our hearts are, we must always give off good energy and do good deeds. What you think is engraved upon you; all your actions are recorded, in space and within yourself.

The Path of Energy

The Himalayan teachings focus inward. In order to deepen our understanding of Yoga, let's take a closer look at the paths of energy (prana) that flow inside our bodies.

As we have mentioned, there are seventy-two thousand invisible paths or nadi within the body, through which life energy, prana, flows. Of these, 108 are particularly important; these are known in China as the meridians of the body, and in Buddhism they are analogues to the 108 earthly desires. We have also mentioned the three most important nadi of all: the nadi of positive energy, pingala; the nadi of negative energy, ida; and the central nadi, Sushumna.

During our lives, the stresses of karma are deposited in these nadi, causing them to clog up. The Sushumna nadi, particularly, is a repository for remnants of karma from past lives, sanskara, etc. By removing these clogs, you will be better able to free yourself from attachments.

There are also seven energy centers, or chakras, in the human body. These are located in the coccyx, the sacral bone, the solar plexus, the chest, the throat, between the brows, and at the very top of the head. These chakras are synced with hormone centers, and if their energy is insufficient, their functioning will weaken, and they will be unable to work properly. The nadi are connected with the chakras, and through them, energy is carried throughout the body.

The seven chakras are the muladhara chakra, the svadisthana chakra, the manipura chakra, the anahata chakra, the vishuddha chakra, the ajna chakra, and the sahasrara chakra. From the lowest level of consciousness to the highest, each has a corresponding "body."

The physical body is also called the earth body. Within it is the emotional body, the water body. There is also the astral body (an invisible, fine body of energy that contains both mind and emotion), the fire body, the mind body, the wind body, and the soul or sound body. Furthermore, there is the cosmic body and the space body as well as the supreme existence body. The chakra of each body uses energy to awaken the consciousness of each. Through purifying by the kriya of Himalayan Yoga, and Anugraha diksha, you can come to know each of these bodies inside and out.

By ordering these energies, awakening all bodies from the physical and mental upward, purifying them, attaining balance, and transcending them all, you can gain a deep wisdom and power, and progress into being a person of inner beauty who is free of all attachments.

Through Himalayan Yoga, the energies that have pooled in various dead-ends and cul-de-sacs here and there, or flowed needlessly elsewhere, will be made to run smoothly and without waste; all will become clear, and you will be awakened.

Techniques for Changing

One secret method, the Anugraha kriya (meditation on light) from a samadhi Yogi, is a technique that directly changes the inner self. To practice this successfully, a thorough knowledge of your internal energy is necessary; to attempt this by yourself can be very dangerous, so please be careful.

Anugraha kriya purifies each energy center and makes it change. For example, within your energy, your earth energy is purified and becomes water energy, which can then go further and become fire. To change from water into fire is to change into something completely different; it is a return to the source and connected with transcending the mind.

This kriya from a samadhi Yogi is different from regular kriya. A Yogi who has achieved samadhi is a person who thoroughly knows everything, has returned to the source existence, and developed their divine energy. Through their power and wisdom, they have the power to change others. The kriya that is born of that power holds wisdom and the divine grace of Anugraha, making it both safe and powerful.

Within kriya are many things such as yoga exercises, breathing methods, pranayama, bandha (yoga that involves tightening the body), mudra (yoga poses involving symbolic hand gestures), etc. There are numerus books on pranayama and other techniques. However, the techniques of Himalayan Yoga are part of a secret Yoga and cannot be experienced through words and books alone. They are accompanied by a profound wisdom and divine grace. To perform these techniques alone, without a samadhi master to guide you, is extremely foolhardy. You may do irreparable damage and find it impossible to restore the balance of your energies. If your practice is particularly poor, you may even struggle to return to normal life. You *must*, therefore, have the guidance of a master to practice Yoga.

Anugraha kriya was born of the wisdom of Himalayan Yogic samadhi. It is a practice of light. Within it, the secret techniques of the Himalayas are taught as the secret kriya meditation technique, and you will receive kriya diksha. Each practitioner is initiated in the way best suited to them and directed to samadhi as quickly as possible. By layering practices, the trash of the heart that is karma is cleaned out naturally and without waste, just as if it were done by a powerful vacuum cleaner.

The Amazing Power Within

If one meditates deeply, and the energies of the mind and body are ordered through continuing practice, then one ceases to dream. However, if you experience a lot during the day, since your consciousness is switched on, the karma within you activates in response. Then, in the world of latent consciousness within, numerous energies wriggle about. The small universes of our minds and bodies hold a variety of untapped powers that are virtually without limit.

I am sure you know of the superhuman strength people can find in emergencies. I refer to the sort of situation where, when a house is on fire, even a frail woman can lift and carry a heavy chest of drawers with ease. In normal life, she thinks she can't, so she doesn't even try. However, in extraordinary circumstances, the power in her latent consciousness comes to life, and she displays amazing strength.

When the mind is concentrated, it can birth enormous power. How fantastic would it be to be able to call on this power in everyday life?

When Chakras Are Activated

It is possible to make mistakes while practicing Yoga, and to create problems for yourself. For example, if you want supernatural powers, and attempt to activate your chakras after reading a book on the subject, you are heading for trouble.

Chakras relate to the nerves and hormones in addition to being places where karma from past lives piles up. If they are manipulated unskillfully, the nerves can become hypersensitized, the various karmas of past lives can activate and once-invisible things become visible, which can make it very difficult to maintain balance. While the mind knows these phenomena are illusory, it can still be buffeted about by them, and leading a normal life can become taxing. Therefore, it is extremely dangerous to mimic Yogic practices on your own or set store in the guidance of an unseasoned master.

Also, developing only one specific part, such as through the covetous mind that desires supernatural powers, is forbidden in Himalayan Yoga. Increased spiritual abilities can serve to expand fear and negative energy, causing many problems. If you purposefully upset the balance of your deepest energies, it can be incredibly difficult for someone to fix.

To reiterate: following a proper master—a samadhi Yogi—and practicing Yoga properly is essential. If you don't, not only will you fail in your quest for enlightenment, but your actions will lead to failure and suffering.

7

What Is God? What Is Karma? God's Existence and Us

In these pages, I have often used the word *God*. Let me, here, explain what I mean. What you were born from, the deep inner existence that creates everything—that is God. It doesn't have an anthropomorphic existence, nor is it imagination created by the human mind. It's probably best to think of it as the great existence that transcends all things.

God is the creator and the sustainer, the existence that supports this world in its entirety. Because of this, it is also called the Supreme Consciousness, or Higher Consciousness, or simply "Existence" (Being). Without God, nothing would be able to live. It can see without eyes, hear without ears. It can go anywhere, even without feet, and make everything, even without hands. It does not have a bodily form, but dwells in every person, animal, and thing.

God could even be called the Mother of the Universe: everything issues from it, is born of it. Its love is like the ocean. God is also energy. If not for the energy of God, water wouldn't run into the sea, and the wind wouldn't blow. Fire wouldn't burn, and flowers, trees, and fruit wouldn't grow. All phenomena in this world are due to the energy of God. If it weren't for this energy, no activity would be possible, and the light of the sun itself would be extinguished.

God Is Embodied in Many Energies

I am aware that some readers of this book may be wary of the word *God*, and that others will reject it outright. If this applies to you, change the word *God* to *all energy* in your head, and try to accept it in that sense.

In Japan, there are said to be eight million gods. There are gods of agriculture, gods of easing birth, gods of education, gods of protection from danger, gods of business prosperity, gods of art, gods of martial arts, and on and on. In India, there are said to be eighty-four thousand gods, and people receive the power necessary for their lives from the god they regard as the source of their energy.

The various gods are the separation of this energy and its embodiment in individual symbols, and the collection of these energies is soul. In other words, the existence known as *you* is a body separated from one great God. It is important, then, while believing in your own essence, to also believe in and respect all of the gods that have been symbolized from that energy. This will lead you onto the path of understanding the microcosm you are.

When you look back on your life up to now, aren't there times when you felt, "Ah, I was protected," or, "I must have had some sort of guidance." Your life was given to you through the many energies called God. By becoming aware of this energy and by concentrating on it, you can awaken to inner power and receive its help.

After the Outer Pilgrimage Is Over

We often make pilgrimages to temples and shrines, and we pray to symbols of God. Himalayan saints and Indian people have gone on pilgrimages to holy places (Gangotri, Kedarnath, Yagunatri, Badrinath, Benares, etc.) for over two millennia, beginning with Mount Kailash in Tibet, said to be the home of Shiva. I too have made pilgrimages to these mountains.

In Japan, pilgrims wearing white clothing undertake the "pilgrim's journey" to the eighty-eight holy sites of Shikoku, which is done over at least forty days. Desiring the salvation of the gods, these pilgrims disengage from everyday life and walk continuously, without interruption. Walking is a very natural movement of the body, and undertaking it with a spiritual mind, leaving idle thoughts behind, cultivates a strong sense of piety. However, the Himalayan teachings urge us not to stop at outward pilgrimage, but to continue with the aim of meeting God within the self.

In India, many people leave home for the purpose of truly meeting the God that is the existence that creates all things. They have hopes such as, "The existence of God is more valuable than anything, I can't die without knowing it," or, "I don't want to die in the darkness, I want to walk into the light." By awakening to the fact that we are given life by the source of all things, and by aligning the energies we receive from this source, we can draw extraordinary qualities out of ourselves.

Gods may be Shinto, Buddhist, Hindu, etc.—they are all, without exception, various names given by various religions and peoples to the primal source and the various energies that manifest from it. These energies are contained in the microcosm inside us; by becoming aware, we are able to return to their source.

You Are God's Shrine

The inner journey I am recommending seems difficult at first glance, but, with the Anugraha Himalaya Samadhi Program, you can step onto the path safely, and proceed at quite a pace.

By receiving and being purified by holy waves, by being purified by Anugraha kriya, and by practicing meditation and prayer, your mind and body become recharged, and you become the shrine of God. Through polishing your mind and body, the holiness of this shrine actually will begin to show. Eventually, you will become a pure and holy person.

Polish your body—your shrine and temple—and put it in order. Then polish your heart to remove all clouds. A diamond's brilliance will well up inside you.

What Is Karma?

Karma can be defined as all mental and physical behavior that derives from our past lives and memories. It is an important and powerful aspect of our lives. Let's look at it more closely.

People give birth to memories through their thoughts, feelings, and actions, and karma is born as a result. While it's true that all living things have feelings, the great difference between people and other animals is that people have minds, buddhi (understanding consciousness), knowledge, and wisdom. We think, forget, decide, act, check, etc.; these are all actions that create karma.

There are several types of karma: *sanskara* is the memory of all past lives that worked to give us birth; *pradabda* is the phenomena that have been drawn into our present and future lives through memories from past lives; and *boga* is karma that operates in the present through our memories of past karma. Our current behavior is also etched in with all of our memories. Our lives are affected by these various types of karma, and we generate new karma for ourselves through subsequent actions. Not everything in life is determined by karma, but new karma that is built up by our daily thoughts and actions can influence what we go on to do next.

For example, even without the connection of marriage in sanskara, if one builds up karma desiring to marry, the request will be granted. This is the law of destiny, the law of karma. If your pradabda is strong, it becomes phenomenalized either in this life or a life to come. If you are currently feeling strong pain or strong happiness, it is a result of pradabda from the past. Familiarity with these karmic laws is useful, as you continue on your journey toward emancipation.

The Truth About Reincarnation

Reincarnation is also known as *rinne tensho*—the circle of transmigration. I believe that reincarnation exists, and that it is directed by karma.

All existence in the universe evolves. It is born and dies, changes form, returns to its source, and is born again. Humans, animals, and plants—all is circulating. The soul does not change, but karma changes; it is given and received. What happens, then, when a person dies? Karma operates before God, and all the memories in the universe act as witnesses, and continue to exist, even after death. All things appear before God, and one's parents are chosen; because of this, the soul of your current existence is connected to your parents in a past life. We are all born to people to whom we have connected in our past, in an attempt to maintain karmic balance.

Sanskara is used in making this selection. Of course, after rebirth, the cycle continues, and contact with parents, through education, the environment, etc., will once again create karma.

Karma Appears and Disappears Without Fail

Karma is born from all of the memories that everyone has, and the behavior of that karma is again remembered and affects the future. Karmic memory from past lives, pradabda, is accumulated as memories which then affect phenomena that occur in our present and future lives. However, we don't know how far into the future these phenomena will occur, just as we don't know how long ago presently occurring karma comes from, or which past life it derives from. No one can predict in which life particular karma will occur. It is not fixed in this way.

Karma appears and disappears without fail. People return, are reborn through sanskara, live with various karma, and die again, during which, both pradabda and boga appear. The circle of life is drawn through these karmic laws.

Plants also have prana (spirit), but when their prana runs out, they simply die without leaving karma behind. The karma in plants is only boga, that of current behavior. The seeds of karma known as sanskara and pradabda are only found in humans. Because of the memories that bring forth karma, we are given opportunities to improve our karma, and to gain good karma. If you wish to become free at rebirth, the solution is to awaken, discard attachment, and live a life that doesn't create karma. If you are able to do this, you can free yourself from the karmic cycle.

If your karma is pure, you will eventually be led to samadhi. When this happens, you will receive eternal life without the repetition of rebirth and become one with God. But until that happens, you will be reborn many times, and receive many opportunities to purify your karma.

Karma from Past Lives

We are packed full of experiences due to karma accumulated through past lives over years of rebirth. Part of this karmic memory is referred to by scientists as DNA. This is comparable to a tiny seed that wishes to someday sprout, spread its leaves, and bloom. The fulfilment of this yearning leads both to its manifestation and the memory of it, which, together, comprise one human life. However, the mysteries of life cannot be explained by DNA alone.

When the results of karma are positive, they bring joy, but this joy also functions as an attachment, which leads to suffering. If there is something negative in a past life, similar negative things will be attracted to present life through the workings of karma. Such things as sickness, accident, and disaster are generally understood as fate, but behind them lies the hidden workings of karma.

It is, of course, beneficial for people to live lives they feel good about living, but we know from experience that this often doesn't go well. This is because we hide many negative things inside us—such things as doubt, anger, and fear. Within these abide experiences from our birth to the present, along with anything that is left over from a past life. If, for example, you tried to obtain something but failed to do so, that painful memory remains.

Memories of this kind can manifest out of the blue. Life is actually a series of such occurrences. The people you meet, the relationships into you enter—all is directed by karma.

When Ingrained Karmic Memories Manifest as Phenomena

Inside you is a mass of karmic results accumulated from past lives that you are not aware of. Your everyday behavior is also born of such things. There is also karma that is activated and expressed by particular circumstances or when certain conditions are brought into alignment by external factors.

Some people, out of boredom, can't control themselves and get into confrontational situations. Others—people of good character, who appear to lead admirable lives—seem always to meet with calamity and disaster, causing us to exclaim, "Why is such a good person so unfortunate?" These types of people, because of memories related to something in the past, have karma that causes misfortune. It is latently remembered by the mind and body even though we may not remember or be aware of it ourselves.

Try to remember that karmic memory is ingrained. When karma is activated, it causes problems, depending on the kind of person you are. Normally, it is quite impossible to change your fate. However, Himalayan esotericism purifies internal karma; by practicing its teachings in earnest, it is possible to free yourself from the karmic cycle.

Testimonial: Making Others Happy Through Meditation

from a nurse in Miyagi

More than three years have passed since my sixty-two-year-old father began to meditate. A salesman, he wakes up before five o'clock almost every morning and immediately works on the samadhi meditation he received from Yogmata. This is the start of his day.

Before beginning meditation, my father was a heavy smoker, smoking two packs a day. At one point, consulting with Yogmata, I said, "My father smokes too much. I can't stand it anymore." Yogmata replied, "That's how your father is balancing himself. It would be great if your father would meditate as well." I thought, "What? That'll never happen!" I couldn't imagine that someone who couldn't take his hands off cigarettes all day long would be able to sit quietly.

However, after considering Yogmata's words, I decided to recommend meditation to my father, and became convinced that he would be able to stop smoking. I talked with my father and told him that Yogmata was willing to talk with him. Sensing his mood change, I invited him to Tokyo, and he replied with a surprisingly calm, "OK." My father didn't tell me what he and Yogmata talked about, but, on the train back to Sendai, I understood that he realized Yogmata respected his feelings.

Then, to my surprise, my father began to practice samadhi meditation, morning and night. He stopped smoking about one year later. It happened naturally: he caught

a cold, stopped smoking, and realized he could live with-
out it. Now his body doesn't get tired as easily, and he feels
fresh and awake in the morning. His diabetes numbers
have improved, even without medication. And, what I'm
most thankful for, for my father as a salesman, is that his
awareness of other people has improved; he no longer gets
nervous and is better able to express his opinions to his col-
leagues. His confidence has grown, he has a good influence
on sales, and he smoothly processes complaints.

Yogmata often says that, when you receive meditation,
you not only become happy yourself, but you make oth-
ers around you happy as well. I hadn't intended to make
others happy, but by doing samadhi yoga, my view of my
father changed, and now he too is changing. It's like throw-
ing a pebble into the water and watching the small ripples
on the surface gradually grow.

Karma Is Also Recorded in the Universe

Some people lament the fact that God sends suffering into
our lives. Others argue that, if God exists, there shouldn't
be any suffering in the world at all. However, it is not God
that creates suffering. Yes, God gave us our minds and
bodies, but it is people who abuse these bodies—through
ignorance, ego, and desire. People burden themselves with
karma, and experience suffering as a result.

All of the karma from our past lives is recorded inside
us; it is also recorded in the universe. The future is created through this karma, and so it is our own minds, not
God, that create suffering. God purifies us and causes us
to evolve, sending us into the world with the words, "Remember your true essence, then return to me."

Humans have been given minds that create things just
as they think them. Also, because our senses have developed to such an extent, we are busy fulfilling our desires,
remaining steadfastly at their mercy, and forgetting the
essential way of life. Not only are we attached to material

things, but we are at the mercy of so much information that the mind inevitably swells. We become bloated with pride.

Then, without having any reason to remember who we really are, ten or twenty years go by in the blink of an eye.

How to Purify Karma

What, then, should be done to purify karma? It isn't easy. But karma can be completely purified only through samadhi; is there no hope, then, for the regular person who has yet to attain enlightenment?

No, there is always hope. The first important thing is to do good deeds to improve your karma. If you continue, good energy will start to accumulate, and can then direct your everyday actions toward good behavior and good thoughts. This accumulation of good energy is referred to as "gaining merit."

The accumulation of good karma is the doing of good deeds that bring no harm to yourself or others, but which bring happiness to both parties. This is giving without seeking reward and serving others. For example, in India, many people go to the temples on Saturdays and Sundays to help with reception and cleanup the place of worship. If they are wealthy, they provide meals in the temples, give alms to those who have been in accidents, help to build new temples, etc. Such service is a very good basis of karma purification. Of the eight stages of Yoga, yama and niyama are necessary for this.

The important thing is to perform service unselfishly, without desire. In our everyday behavior, we are accustomed to acting only in the interest of our desires, but service doesn't expect anything in return; it is a release only. One sees similar elements in many volunteer activities, but you must be careful, as such activities often lead to a strengthening—a swelling—of the ego. Such activities do not help to purify karma. Purification must be a devotion of one's deeds to God, a purification of karma through action—that is, deeds done only for the purpose of unification with your original existence; deeds that cause your consciousness to evolve.

Acting in such a way results in the natural accumulation of merit and positive energy, and the filling of one's self with good waves. This causes bad waves to decay and fall away. It should be stressed that this training is only possible because we have physical bodies; it is essential to train and purify your karma while you are living.

We are born and we die, and we come back to the world again and are given opportunities to further our purification. Failure, sickness, and difficulty also take form for the purpose of karmic release and purification, for our growth. We continue to come back to this world, time and time again, until we become masters of enlightenment. Our return to this world is only for the purpose of purifying karma; rebirth is an opportunity given to us by God.

Without purifying ourselves, neither the eternal life known as moksha nor the attainment of enlightenment are possible. Until enlightenment is attained, until one achieves samadhi and attains to moksha, rebirth occurs many, many times.

Meditation Methods for Purifying Karma Quickly

Himalayan esotericism can purify karma quickly. Among its methods, Anugraha, diksha, and instruction in secret meditation can purify you quickly and easily, without effort, even in the same day. Through diksha from a master, you receive divine waves that awaken you inside and purify karma. Kripa is also effective—Anugraha from a master that functions as a catalyst or bridge.

Anugraha and diksha will make you feel as though you are dancing in midair. The inner restriction, the tightening of one's mind due to karma, quickly changes through reception of blessings and diksha and through doing samadhi meditation. Additionally, if you practice kriya meditation and are able to expand your awareness, your karma will be further purified.

There are many types of people in the world, and they hold many different values. Karmic memory is stimulated as a result, and its activity begins. Our various encounters bring up that which is hidden inside ourselves, providing opportunities for awareness and purification. Through training, you will be able to separate from the mind of like and dislike, attain a free spirit, grow into a person of universal love, and become a more vital, more abundant, you. You will be given the opportunity to practice a new way of living.

When bad things happen as the result of karma from previous lives, it is important to regard them as opportunities for study. Try to be grateful for them, and, with awareness, continue on to further good actions. By carrying this good energy, you will progress on the path toward your true self. Eventually, you will no longer produce karma; it will disappear, and you will be released.

Knowing the Appropriate Use of the Physical Body

Illness and aging cause us pain. However, these are also things that are caused by karma. If we can purify our karma, we become less susceptible to illness and better able to keep aging in check.

Why do our bodies become sick in the first place? This is due to karma, because of fatigue due to only using certain parts of the body, as a result of some imbalance or shock in past lives or in this life, and due to an increase of imbalances caused by the flow of irregular energy in the areas that received the shock. Just as karma differs from person to person, so do imbalances and fatigued areas differ.

Illness often progresses at a level we remain unaware of. Weak digestive systems, weak hearts, weak livers, weak kidneys, weak eyes, chronic disease—all have karma as the cause. If you suffer from such an ailment, you must purify the karma of your mind and body and strengthen any areas that have gone unused. Try to achieve a natural balance and develop the skills to be able to deeply relax.

If you constantly use the same parts of the body, you become overly reliant on those particular circuits, so that you don't know how to give them a rest. This is a kind of excitement at the cellular level. This not only applies to the mind and body, but to diet, environment, etc. Once things become distanced from nature, and you struggle to maintain balance or to rest, confusion and calamity are usually not far away.

For example, early spring is hay fever season, and various allergies and illnesses appear. Those who suffer do their best to counter them, but they don't go away easily. This is because the body is in an unusual state of excitement due to karma and the environment.

To better prevent illness of the body and mind, you must restore your essential power of judgment. Try to be aware of what is right and what is disharmonious. Try to achieve harmony within yourself.

Testimonial: Samadhi Meditation Guides Me
from a corporate manager in Tokyo

I used to steel myself with the idea that men must put their all into work, and that I had to do everything myself. In a management position at a software development company, there are many things to determine and decide, and I was constantly anxious and hesitant about whether a judgment or decision was correct and about what to do if it wasn't. I did my best to overcome these feelings, but there were times when I felt tired or empty, or simply wanted to give up.

Then I met Yogmata and began samadhi meditation out of a desire to become stronger spiritually. I participated in seminars and training camps, received individual sessions, and gradually became more involved. Through daily meditation, I became able to calm myself.

After about six months, I suddenly began to feel many changes. In software development, it's very difficult to search for engineers who meet project requirements, but I'd be contacted by engineers at just the right time or, when I was looking for them, I'd find them right away.

As my meditation deepened, work naturally began to go well. Even in cases where I couldn't get an order, the particular project would turn out to be troublesome and I realized I was fortunate that it hadn't worked out after all.

In a seven-day training camp, during meditation, I felt a swirling whiteness centered within myself, as if I'd become one with energy itself. A beam of light entered the tip of my head and spread through my body, becoming a sphere of energy. My body went into another dimension, time and space disappeared, and Yogmata was right there beside me. The more I stayed centered, the more the energy throbbed, and I felt that I could be free. Finally, my head became very clear and scenes such as that of completing work at amazing speed flowed through at breakneck speed, faster than thought. I felt truly changed and was very moved.

Samadhi meditation has become an indispensable part of my daily life. It guides me and brings me happiness. At work, I no longer think of unnecessary things, my decisions have become quick and accurate, and even in jobs that I might think of as burdensome, a lifeboat almost always appears. It's really mysterious. My worries about the future have completely disappeared.

I have new ideas for software and business models and am more creative in general. I feel as though I'm riding a flow, and the flow is constantly getting bigger. It's very mysterious!

Preparation from the Original Energy

If you want to prevent illness and aging, you must keep your body in proper balance and get deep rest. Also, as you let go of everything, you should transmit life force to underused areas to revive them and try to calm those areas that are abnormally excited.

If abnormally excited areas are left unchecked, abnormal things like cancer cells may develop. For example, if you continue with a lifestyle in which you eat unnatural foods in an unnatural environment, irrepressible excitement develops at the cellular level, putting your body at risk.

In order to prevent such things, it is necessary to know what part of the body or mind is being used disproportionately. If the mind is in the habit of blaming the self or others, if it becomes spoiled, stubborn, dissatisfied, or uneasy, then many internal or external stresses may result, such as those that affect the stomach, uterus, and liver. When the symptoms of disease appear, it is often already too late. As preventive medicine, it is necessary to constantly return to nature while coming to know the self.

At this point, I think you can appreciate the very big effect that karma has on illness and aging, and that it is related to society. The mysterious workings of the human body cause us to grow and offer us protection, but, over time, they are broken down by the ego. Real wisdom and true life science about the human body are not taught to us in modern society.

Certainly, doctors are often excellent at locating pathogens, ulcers, and cancer. However, ulcers and cancer are already well advanced by the time they can be seen, and by this time it is often the case that only symptomatic treatment is possible. However, if we have already identified karma as the ultimate cause, we can prevent these things before they become serious illnesses.

Before our physical bodies were formed, we had a fine, invisible astral body and, in addition, a fine energy body, called a causal body. These bodies contain all of the information recorded from past lives—in other words, sanskara and pradabda karma. It is crucial, then, to purify at this level, and to correct any imbalances we detect.

The power of Anugraha, of mantra and pratyahara, and the secret method of kriya, can bring about this transformation. Through the secret methods of Yoga, you can prepare your body and mind and experience great healing in trust, gratitude, and love, receiving help in purifying the memories of the astral body.

However, I must repeat that these methods of preparing the body from within are not taught in schools or society. Yes, we often hear about the benefits of running and similar forms of exercise, but no one teaches why this prevents illness or what type of exercise would be appropriate for a particular person.

The important thing to realize is that it is your mind that governs your body, and that your mind can further your physical symptoms or habits. By becoming aware, you will be able to use your body and mind correctly and connect to the God that gave them life.

8

Mind, Body, and Soul: The Painful Thoughts of Those Who Choose Suicide

"I'm tired of living. I'm sorry. I'm weak." There are people who choose suicide, and who leave such notes behind. I have been told that the number of suicides in Japan exceeds thirty thousand per year, a comparatively high rate among the world's population, and more than the number of those killed in traffic accidents.

There are those who become so trapped or burdened by their lives, whose lives become so painful that, in suffering and greatly troubled, they choose death. If they could ask friends or family for help, things would go well but their egos prevent them from doing so. Perhaps some had led a relatively blessed life up until the point when problems occurred: debt, failure, lack of hope for the future, the sense of no way out.

There are people with weak personalities who, meeting with harsh criticism or under other kinds of attack, are unable to endure the pain and choose suicide. They are caught up in the idea that everything will end with death, that they will be released from their suffering.

I cannot emphasize too strongly the fact that suicide, as an action, ignores the natural power without which we wouldn't be able to live. It is the intentional severing of karma. Unable to think of the next life they will live, people who choose suicide only think of the present.

If you take your own life, not only will those you leave behind be troubled, but your own soul will be troubled as well. The memory of the pain of suicide is etched in the fine body called the astral, and, further, it is recorded in the soul's home, the fine body called the causal, where it becomes sanskara. At this point, you cannot be reborn soon. Barred from heaven, you become a phantom, wandering this way and that, troubling others.

Even After Suicide, the Soul Doesn't Die

Those who contemplate suicide used to have hope for the future, until their thinking became negative and they lost the energy or will to continue. They fret about losing something and the ego of fear appears.

Some people feel guilty: "I've made mistakes in the world; I can't face people or society." Guilt will go to great lengths to plague a person. Even though they may not have done anything wrong, an obstruction appears in their minds and they feel pain even though they aren't the cause.

Causing suffering to friends and family also causes suffering to the self. The person contemplating suicide may think, "If I'm alive, the people around me suffer. If I disappear, everyone's pain will stop. If I don't exist, things will be peaceful, and others will be able to have happiness." Perhaps we can persuade ourselves that "for the sake of others" reflects the workings of a sound mind. But it in no way purifies karma.

Life is a precious, important thing. God didn't send people into the world for them to take their own lives. People should live in nature and die having lived fulfilled lives. A great scar is left when a life given for the purpose of living is cut short because of the mind's erroneous judgment, or because of the ego. We must all protect others from this behavior, if we are to save them.

When Someone Takes Their Life, The Soul Suffers

Those who plan suicide are fundamentally mistaken. The mistake lies in the conviction that everything stops when life is cut off. If you commit suicide, the world is still there. The world that existed before you persists, and the mind doesn't disappear simply because the body dies. The suffering of the mind doesn't stop. The mind's memories and awareness are still there. Prana, and the power to think, remain in the astral body.

Because of this, the soul experiences great suffering after suicide. Of course, the act itself creates great trauma. Then the astral body, laden with suffering, becomes a phantom, wandering to and fro. Moreover, a phantom is loved by no one and has no home. Ancestors do not welcome the soul of one who has committed suicide.

I say again: we weren't born in order to commit suicide. We were born to give love. Our bodies are gifts from God. We were given bodies in order to grow and become aware of the truth in this world. If this world is not to your liking, change the way that you live in this world! If you can't love people, first come to love yourself.

Put All Your Effort into Doing What You've Been Given to Do Now

People suffer in order to create things. When new encounters happen, when we make things, when we grow, when we're born—these are always accompanied by suffering. People are born after suffering. So we can't allow ourselves to be defeated by suffering. Rather, we should change ourselves.

Rather than think of suicide, change the mind and be born anew. Suicide doesn't only harm the body; it harms the mind and soul and leaves a record of pain in one's own mind, and in the minds of family and friends. This all becomes karma—bad karma—that will inevitably come into play.

The thoughts of the ego that suggest suicide may give birth to a feeling of happiness that one may temporarily escape suffering, but this is by no means a victory for the self. At the moment you think of suicide, you must change yourself.

Rather than consign yourself to death, you must use your body and mind and become a creative person with new ideas. If you have the strength to throw it all away, I urge you to redirect that strength and join me.

It takes a change of mind to think about how one is to live in this world and how one is to do new things. Rather than sticking to one thing, release it and change. Give change to your body and give change to your mind; transform from within.

It's not easy, I know, to change the mind in an instant. At first, it is essential that you connect to power of a high dimension. It is also essential to practice on a daily basis; if you do so, no matter how difficult it is, you will overcome the difficulties that face you, through the support of the source that makes you alive.

Our bodies and minds are given to us for our growth— we don't own them, as such. It is important that we put our effort into that which we have been given to do. This is done by unifying the three energies of body, mind, and soul with awareness and no mind. The thoughts of your mind are not you, so let them go. Then purify and transform. If you do this, your ego will vanish, and a chink will open in the mind. Through meditation, this can happen very quickly.

Yagya, the fire ritual, can also help your awareness transform, and can even change the fate of others. If someone close to you, or of one of your ancestors, committed suicide, hold a memorial service for them. Through the transforming energy of Yagya, the universe's energy will shift.

The Relationship between Mind, Body, and Soul

"I understand mind and body. But what, exactly, is the soul?" Many people ask this question. The soul can be thought of as God's alter ego; it is a part of God, an existence comprised of the same nature as God. Body and mind were sent into this world from that soul.

The body is something that was created based on an element called *prakriti*, the source of matter. Prakriti also manifests as five elements: air, wind, fire, water, and earth. These blend, and things with form are created from that which is without form.

The mind is born from the soul. In the mind is born *asumita* (the awareness of I), resulting in *ankara* (the ego), then *chida* (awareness), and *buddhi* (understanding consciousness). The mind is stimulated by the senses and has various experiences. It also has many functions, such as understanding these experiences, expressing emotion, memory, etc. The mind's power is stronger than anything. Depending on how the mind is cared for, it can become a mind of selfish egoism or a social mind. If it is well controlled, the ego will drop away, and it will develop into a universal mind.

The soul differs from the mind, and the essential self is nothing other than the soul. In other words, the soul, with its sunlike existence, supports and transmits energy to all. Most people live in a state in which the mind sustains the soul: their minds are overdeveloped and have become convinced that they are in fact the self. In order to be free from all, it is necessary to transform back into the soul that is God's alter ego. This is becoming one's true self, a process called self-realization.

In managing these aspects of ourselves—mind, body, and soul—it is important to have a universal love that transcends individuality, to be grateful for all phenomena, and to exist without becoming attached to phenomena. If you achieve this, you can step back and take a cool look at your rejoicing self.

If we change our awareness in this way, the body changes, the mind changes—everything changes. Even if you don't feel it right away, as purification progresses, you will gradually feel a real improvement. Through sleeping better, you will become more efficient during the day, and will make better use of your essential abilities and inherent skills. If you can do this, not only will you become happy, but your family and those around will also become happy. By changing your awareness, the cycle of virtue is passed along.

The Mind's Memory Remains in the Spirit

In the world of spirituality, the word *spirit* is often used separately from soul. What, exactly, is the spirit? The spirit is the mind and the soul. It isn't something that only comes into existence at death; it resides in the body while we're alive. When the body passes away at death, the mind and soul depart the body as spirit. Karma remains in the spirit in the form of sanskara, which works for the purpose of rebirth, and prarabdha, which causes future phenomena.

What is called the soul in English is called Atman in Sanskrit. Without karma, it is essentially pure—the alter ego of God, free of all memories of the mind. It's fine to think of spirit as being the mind, with its karma, and the soul together. The spirit is also called the spirit body, or the astral body. However, please note that, in Christianity, the word spirit is used to refer to the soul. When we follow Himalayan theory, ghost and the spirits of ancestors are also spirits. Angels, too, can be called a type of spirit. Angels are divine energy sent to help us.

Enlightenment purifies the karma and results in a soul of divine quality. Spirits don't approach those who are enlightened. However, they desire salvation, and will appear for those who have an interest in them.

Do So-Called Heaven and Paradise Exist?

Talk of heaven and hell is found in any religion—in Christianity, Islam, Buddhism, and Hinduism, among others—and in myths, legends, and folklore around the world. Heaven and hell are also mentioned in the "prana" of Indian mythology. It is said that, if you commit crimes in this world, you will fall into hell after death, but that, if you do good deeds, help others, and give alms, you will go to heaven.

Even in the afterlife, in the disembodied state before rebirth—that is, in the state of existence as spirit—we are tortured by the various manifestations of karma. At death, the fine, invisible astral body slips out of the physical body, and it is possible to see, at once, all of the things you have experienced up to that point, as if looking at a revolving lantern. Everything is recorded in the astral body. At death, it separates from the physical body, and, in the process of becoming spirit, if there are various attachments in the mind, or if the ego is hardened, it suffers when the body dissolves and returns to the elements.

It is said that, even after becoming spirit, the God of Hell gives us a body for suffering—we are made to suffer according to our karma. In other words, if we don't purify our karma, much suffering awaits us after death. The important thing is that there is no physical body after death. After death, you cannot train and purify. After death, you cannot attain enlightenment.

Heaven and Hell Are Right There Beside You

Heaven and hell are by no means places that we only go to after death. We have been given our bodies, and heaven and hell exist in the midst of our various circumstances.

I am very fortunate: I love people, I am loved in return, and I don't experience suffering. Not only that, but I am blessed with abilities and good health. To live life in such a way is truly heavenly.

On the other hand, there are people who are unlucky: even though they have not done anything wrong, they always get hurt or unconsciously hurt others. Or they are stressed by mental distress and feel sorrow. Or they are always obsessed with worries of illness and possibly suffer from the effects of surgery. This is just like being in hell.

There are others, of course, who are not so lucky: people with mental instability or physical injury, people who are forever experiencing sorrow and distress even though they haven't done anything wrong. This is the suffering of hell.

What should be done in order to separate from such a hellish world and go to heaven? The answer is clear: awaken to truth, know the truth of your body and mind, and live with awareness. When this is accomplished, you are free, and able to live without being at the mercy of karma. Such a life is full of compassion, gratitude for everything, and natural existence in a heavenly manner.

It is also possible to see heaven in the process of samadhi—you can have various experiences as your meditation deepens. Rich visions can be seen in the process of purifying the five elements (earth, water, fire, wind, and air). Also, you become air (void, empty) by purifying your karma; this gives you a feeling of weightlessness, of having no body, during which you can see beautiful visions.

The road to samadhi is a return journey to the existence of the source that created all things. Samadhi experience, transcending the physical body to become the astral and then the cosmic body, is the very experience of heaven.

Our Existence Comes from the Source

That we were given life in this world is by no means accidental. By the will of God, the original existence, we have journeyed into this world from a place that cannot be seen with the eyes.

In order to experience truth, your soul, which came from the universe, came to the earth as a traveler. Then, it took existence in form, and now it continues to grow through learning, and lives in order to become a person of abundance. You become one with God through becoming enlightened to truth, becoming one with your soul, and becoming one with existence. Your love becomes one with universal love—this is samadhi. If you know and follow this mechanism, you can become existence itself, power itself, and wisdom itself, without suffering or confusion, and become free from all bondage.

If you can change the programming known as karma through enlightenment, you can change your destiny. Even if you have lived up to now by simply floating along, you can change to live the way you yourself choose by being aware of the world of the source. This path of return to your true self is the path to samadhi; it is the path to satori, self-realization, and enlightenment.

The path to samadhi can also be described as a journey that transcends death. There is nothing to fear. Death is a process that allows you to be born anew, and through which you become your true self. Through it, you can attain enlightenment and become free.

Light and Sound in the Universe

Everything in the universe was born of light and sound. Then, through this sound and through this light, we will return to the source. Even our existence was born of light and sound. As you know, if matter is crushed more and more finely, it eventually becomes invisible molecules, and then atoms. Atoms are made of electrons, protons, and mesons, and, still further, of subatomic particles, fine material that further becomes waves. These waves are light and sound.

Take thunder and lightning: first, there is a spark of light, and then we hear a rumbling sound. If, through samadhi meditation, you shower in these waves of sound and are able to make your mind one with the sound, you can be freed from worldly thoughts and your mind will become still. Then, you will be able to balance your mind and body.

The singing of hymns, uniting the mind with holy waves, is a good way to balance mind and body. Reciting it inside or outside of ourselves is called chanting. When the strings of a guitar are plucked, the sound echoes in the body cavity of the guitar, which expands the waves, resulting in a bigger sound. Chanting does the same thing with your body.

Think of your mouth as analogous to the opening in the guitar, and your body as the hollow cavity. If you softly and slowly say, "U-O-A-E-I," your whole body is massaged, from the back of your mind to your spine, stomach—everywhere. This is one of the effects of chanting. When the words are a prayer, the chant becomes a song of prayer, and when the words are a story, it becomes a type of song called a *bajan*.

If we follow what sounds we hear all the way back we arrive at the sound of the source. If you plant the seed of that sound within, you will become sound itself. Then you too can return, borne along on the waves, to the source from which the sound is born. This is oneness (harmony in unity).

Praising Pure Consciousness

Indian people have deep faith, and, from a young age, they align a channel to a level of consciousness that transcends the human and give praise to God—another form of chanting. By calling the name of God and singing with love, a strong, pure love is called forth.

Thousands of years ago there was a great god named Shiva, who meditated in the Himalayas. Shiva is the deified energy of Nirvana, and the inventor of yoga and meditation. The consciousness of Shiva is extremely pure, and an energy of precisely this purity is within you as well.

Himalayan esotericism contains words of prayer and praise to many gods and holy sages. Anyone who praises feels better: when you speak good words, the positive waves return to you. This is because the recipient of your words becomes happy and returns good feeling. Conversely, if you speak ill of people, they will speak ill of you in return. The waves are paid back in kind.

Use words to adjust the balance of your mind and body. It has long been said that, "Keeping silent about things makes one swell." By using our voices, we can release energy and feel refreshed.

By making the sound, "Aah," the belly becomes empty, like a piece of bamboo. If you use your voice as though your body is a musical instrument, the sound waves will wash your whole body, even down to the cellular level, and you will become clean, as if you have taken an internal shower.

Using our voices also has the benefit of making us into people who can clearly express themselves. Furthermore, breathing in with power results in deep respiration, so oxygen is fully spread through the body and the internal organs are massaged, promoting health.

9

Returning to the True Self Through Meditation: The Process of Transformation

The Importance of Meditation in Life

The ultimate purpose of life is enlightenment. That is, the true meaning of living is to become aware of your true self. This is being where you are now, without going anywhere—the return to the essential self.

The trouble is, we always want to go somewhere! We are always searching for something. Our desires pull us this way and that, and we move around, wandering aimlessly, unable to settle down. Meditation is the transformation of this feeling, training the mind to become empty. It is being here, now, simply being still, without moving. Through meditation, you can unfetter your body and mind. Blood will begin to concentrate in the brain rather than in the body. If you close your eyes, you will feel that the energy which had formerly been leaking to the outside is now starting to build up inside.

The brain that had formerly been tense will relax, brain activity will be stimulated, and purification will occur. Your ears will soon cease to hear external voices, and your consciousness will no longer be directed outward. Then you will be able to hear the inner voice, and the ears will also become activated and purified.

In daily life, there are times when stimuli received over the course of the day, or excitement over some phenomenon, appear that night in our dreams. In the same way, obsessions can rise up during meditation. Just as suppressed things are released in our dreams, so our hidden obsessions and thoughts can suddenly appear during meditation. This is nothing to be surprised by, or worried about. Meditation is a process of purification, and a process of becoming aware of the self. Through it, you will gradually achieve inner tranquility.

Maha Yoga Breathing Meditation Method

Breathing, as a phenomenon, is located between consciousness and unconsciousness. By directing the consciousness toward the breath, you become aware of inner things, and can achieve inner balance. The following breathing method is a meditation that balances various energies and promotes awareness and tranquility.

Maha Yoga Breathing Meditation Method

This meditation should be done in a relaxed position, in a pleasant and enjoyable manner. Choose a quiet place that has good airflow. Use a cushion or towel, if you want, to avoid discomfort. Remove your watch and any accessories, and wear clothing that allows freedom of movement.

Sit in a comfortable position.
Place both hands on your knees, palms facing down.
Close your eyes.
Extend your spine and relax your shoulders.
Focus your awareness on your exhalations and inhalations.
You will be led to a wonderful, tranquil world.
When five minutes have passed, stretch and open your eyes.

Training for Absence of Thought

You can achieve eternal life and true happiness by transcending death and attaining enlightenment. But, to do this, you must remove the darkness inside. A daily meditation practice will cleanse negative thoughts and free up energy.

There are many ways to meditate, but almost all of them are methods of concentration. To progress in your meditation, it is helpful to fix your mind on something and concentrate on it. It could be God, or an element of nature such as a mountain or ravine. mountain or ravine. By concentrating on something external, you are brought inside of yourself and you can proceed with internal concentration.

Then by concentrating on your breath, your vibrations, your energy centers and your love, you can go into meditation. Just synchronize yourself with those things, feel the synchronization completely and then everything will start to disappear.

Concentrate on your breath and your energy centers. Concentrate on love and enter meditation. As the objects of your concentration separate and disappear, you will enter a state of deep meditation in which you are no longer captivated by anything. This is emptiness. You have become free of worldly thoughts.

Breathe Idle Thoughts into the Void

During meditation, the stubborn, stiff, and unmoving parts inside you melt away. Various thoughts float up and vanish; bad thoughts are washed away. The mind itself, which is energy, also vanishes. The path to enlightenment lies in the purification and annihilation of all thoughts. Of course, good thoughts also arise during meditation, and extrasensory perceptions may also manifest. There are those who strive after such results. However, on the true path to enlightenment, these are idle thoughts, and should be released.

By continuing to meditate, everything will ultimately be absorbed in the void (emptiness). This is the form in which the root of thought is annihilated. Then, one becomes no-mind, empty of mind. Even in this state, idle thoughts can still arise; each time this happens, you must release the thought.

Having idle thoughts arise is by no means negative. Becoming aware of the existence of such thoughts is a step forward. These thoughts have been there all along; becoming aware of them now is a result of directing your consciousness inward. Through meditation, these thoughts will arise and disappear like steam, and be replaced by stillness.

Experiencing Absence of Thought

Our minds are filled to bursting with information. Once thoughts begin to be drawn out, thoughts of all kinds—good and bad—appear endlessly, in rapid succession. It can be troublesome when so much concern and worry are drawn out of the mind—the body's condition can be affected, and sometimes worsen, in the confusion. People try various things to remedy this: they have massages or take medicines, or pile on additional external stimuli.

Such things can help temporarily, but they are only symptomatic. When the body is in poor condition, the cause isn't only located in the body; in the majority of cases, the causes are a complex mixture of psychological and functional elements, in which the mind plays a significant part.

If you want to heal from the source, the mind has to be empty. Emptying the mind eliminates worry, and, if you are relaxed spiritually, the body's illnesses will start to disappear. Becoming empty, then, is the removal of polluting thoughts; it is an extremely valuable thing.

Through meditation, you can release everything and become free. Pure love will appear within you, and you will be able to accomplish anything. You will blaze brilliantly with life, and your glow will have a positive effect on those around you.

You will be here, now, in this instant, doing nothing, not going anywhere. This is pure being which creates no karma—the path back to the essential you.

The Process of Change Through Meditation

Inside your body exists the element of earth, which dissolves and becomes fluid. You also contain the element of water, which softens the body and mind. Water then becomes fire. For example, if you put butter into fire, it becomes fluid and begins to burn. When you put food into the body, it is digested and becomes liquefied. Then it is absorbed in the intestines and the body becomes hot—it burns and releases energy.

The burning edge of the flame flickers back and forth and becomes wind. Thoughts are also airy and become wind. Finally, this wind is absorbed into emptiness and becomes emptiness.

The process of change from things that can be seen with the eyes to original existence—the return to existence at the source of creation—is the experience of Anugraha Himalaya Samadhi Program meditation. It is the path to satori, the path to enlightenment.

Testimonial: Meditation Has Made Childbearing Easy and Fun

from a mother in Tokyo

One day, after I had learned meditation, I woke up in the morning and saw my children as angels and was momentarily stunned. Up until that point I had thought my children were cute, but this was the first time that I felt love from the bottom of my heart. It wasn't that I thought, "Children are a gift from heaven," in my head—I felt it from the bottom of my heart. Of course, I still get angry and frustrated with my children from time to time, but I always connect to the existence of love, and that love recharges me so I can immediately return to my original state.

When I hear the tragic news of suicides caused by suffering over a child's illness, or parents who, unable to cope, kill their children, I feel very distressed. I wonder if I might have ended up in such a situation, if I hadn't been fortunate enough to meet Yogmata.

My children also meditate and are connected to Yogmata, so I always have peace of mind. My children possess something akin to religious belief, which, it seems to me, is increasingly rare these days. They have a sense of reverence toward God (or the universe, or nature, if you prefer). We value our own lives as well as the lives of others, and we don't put down or hurt other people. We know that we aren't living through our own power, but that we have been given life; we feel neither inferior nor superior toward others.

My children will soon hit puberty, and I am sure many things will happen, but I feel calm and prepared, because of the peace of mind we enjoy as parent and children. I want mothers who may be experiencing hardship and suffering to know about this fun and enjoyable way of raising children.

Inner Peace Meditation

This is a method of creating tranquility and peace of mind. Where, exactly, is our breath centered, and how does it connect to the center of the universe? This meditation is done while focusing on these things.

Inner Peace Meditation

This inner peace meditation is ideal for image training and can stabilize the mind. The mind becomes detached, serenity is born, and harmony of the body and mind is achieved.

Sit in a comfortable position.

Place both hands on your knees, palms facing down.

Close your eyes.
Focus awareness on your breath as you exhale through
the nose. Focus only on the breath being exhaled,
not the breath being inhaled.
(Inhale as well, of course.)
Focus awareness on how your body is connected to
the center of the universe.
When five minutes have passed, stretch and open your
eyes.

No More Needless Fear and Detours

When there is pain somewhere in the body and we yell
"Ouch!" we only increase the pain. Sometimes we become
overly caught up in the workings of the mind, because of
pain. At such times, it can be helpful to entrust yourself to
the divine waves, the existence that transcends the mind,
through meditation. If you look at your pain while you
meditate, it will disappear.

Pain is just one example. As your meditation practice
progresses you will become aware that you hurt yourself
or attacked others due to an obsession with meaningless or
trifling things. Perhaps you will notice things that you did
out of good intentions, but which were in fact ridiculous.
Or perhaps you will feel silly for having treated yourself
to something lavish that is of absolutely no importance.

Meditation will introduce you to a more vibrant way of
living that will allow you to discover the abundance inside
yourself. It is the work of becoming aware of truth, of
annihilating your various desires. By continuing to meditate, fullness, satisfaction, peace, and joy will overflow
from the innermost depths of your heart.

Also, meditation functions as a kind of energy conserva-
tion: you will find that you can achieve maximum results
with minimum effort. People who don't meditate tend to
be swayed by wasteful desires, do unnecessary things, and

become overanxious and overtired—they expend a great deal of energy and only get minimal results.

Drop Habits and Return the Mind and Body to Their Natural State

People today are unable to recover their energy sufficiently through sleep. The essential function of sleep is to relax the body and mind, replenish energy, and return us to our original state. Adequate sleep allows tired or injured bodies and minds to be restored to their natural state. Most people today, however, expend a lot of energy on their desires, and don't get enough sleep to still their excitement. The complications and artificiality of modern life, and the preponderance of unnatural and processed foods, don't help.

Also, the impression of every behavior becomes memory and is etched into the mind and body. The stress of experience is added to this, and becomes residual, fixed within. To dissolve this, it is essential to meditate every day, in the morning and at night. By doing wave meditation and kriya meditation, you can reflect on the center of the body, reflect on the center of the mind, and return to a pure existence. Then your awareness will deepen, everything will become harmonious, and you will return to your essential self. You will become a stranger to fatigue.

In this world, the things that cause us the most suffering are desire and ignorance. Many desires that seem necessary become absolutely unnecessary when we stop and think about them a little. These desires can be peeled away through meditation. Desire is awakened when the mind turns to nonessentials. However, if you can center yourself through meditation, desire naturally falls away. Then the mind will become pure and truth will appear.

It is essential to purify and release karma if you are to attain enlightenment, but, even with a regular meditation practice, this would take many lifetimes. However, this normally lengthy process can be safely expedited through the secret teachings of Himalayan esotericism. With the help of a samadhi Yogi, your karma can be cleansed surprisingly quickly.

Meditation Is Also Practice to Skillfully Transcend Death

Our minds are tied to that which we love. This is called attachment, but if you die while holding on to attachment—in other words, if you die carrying karma—you will go directly into the world of desire. This becomes suffering after death.

Because of this, I urge you to release your attachments while you are alive and become free before you die. I want you to do good deeds and think good thoughts every day, cleanly purify your karma, meditate, and empty your mind. Meditation brings everything to stillness and makes a new beginning from it. It is a practice of transcending life and transcending death, or, to put it another way, it gives us new life daily.

By deeply resting your mind and body, by making your breathing so shallow that it appears to stop, you will realize, "Oh, death isn't scary either." Then, you will be able to live a truly abundant life. Meditation is truly the basis for living a good life.

Through meditating, you will transcend time and space, and, ultimately, become immortal. Within the profound rest that meditation affords is an inner awakening—a vibrant life.

Know That Everything Has an Outside and an Inside

Are you familiar with the Rorschach test? It is a psychological test involving ambiguous black ink shapes on white paper, in which you are tested on what you see. For example, you might see a beautiful woman, or a very old, wrinkled woman. Perhaps what you see is conditioned by the thoughts you carry inside.

In the same way, there are two sides to everything, depending on your point of view. You may say you're only happy when you're eating good food or with someone you love. However, if you eat without cease, you will become ill, and, no matter how much you love a person, you may occasionally tire of them if you are with them constantly.

There is an inside and outside to everything, and we should know this. But, when we are at the mercy of our obsessions, we can only see the inside *or* the outside. If we are attached to someone we love, we only see their outside. If we find the work we have been given to do boring, we only see its inside.

However, everything has an inside *and* an outside. Those who only see the inside must, through meditation, practice seeing things positively. Those who only see the outside must become aware of the inside as well. If you fail to do this, you will constantly be at the mercy of the mind of like and dislike, and you will not know peace.

Even if you think you hate yourself, you still have to spend every day with yourself. Rather than continuing to hate yourself, you need to relearn how to love yourself. Through meditation, you will come to love yourself.

A Method to Clear Away Wrongdoing and Dirt

Most Japanese people have seen a Shinto priest swish a gohei (a staff with plaited paper streamers) to perform a purification ceremony. This action symbolizes the sweeping away of wrongdoing and impurity. I was interested to notice a similar action when I witnessed a prana remedy in the United States. Water had been placed in a washbasin, and a healer waved his hands in front of the participants and moved his hands quickly as if he was throwing away the dirt into the basin. With the naked eye, I couldn't tell if the water was taking the impurities or if they were being scattered, but this was clearly being done in order to adjust the prana of the participants.

There is also the method of writing down the things you dislike on a piece of paper and then burning the paper to clear impurities and remove the grime from the mind. There are many methods of purifying the mind—the giving of alms is another. The desires of the mind are the root of all heaviness, and the giving of alms releases attachment and lightens the mind.

Samadhi meditation and kriya meditation are very effective methods of lightening the mind. When you meditate, you understand that the source of heaviness is desire, and the mind becomes clear, as if you are swimming without effort in the midst of clear air. In comparison, regular life is akin to desperately wading through thick, heavy mud.

As we have discussed, while the mind is in the process of disliking, it tends to attract dislike to itself, very much like a magnet. If a person's mind is overly developed, this can be especially pronounced. Our interests, also, attract useless dust and junk that is of no consequence. It is useful to be able to swim through such things; if you can't, you pick up dirty clumps of karma. Even if these clumps grow big and heavy, you don't know how to remove them. Think of a dog that shakes itself to fling water off; we, too, need to cleanse ourselves in this way.

I purify people and help them to be able to meditate well as quickly as possible.

Meditate Daily, a Little at a Time, with the Feeling of Brushing Your Teeth

When you meditate, you come to be at ease, and, at the same time, you intuitively understand what other people need. This enriches your relations with others.

Meditation is medicine for the mind, soul, and body—the medicine of invisible waves of holy sound and light. When this medicine starts to work, the ego tries to resist, and there may be times when you feel pain. Some might feel it is not working, but it is working slowly.

Eventually, your body weight will drop, and you will become fit, your figure will improve, and your mind will become light and easy. Everything you eat will taste delicious, and people you dislike will melt away. You will behold the world with happiness and be able to comprehend all.

Then, if you polish your inner self, your talent will naturally bloom. Interestingly, this internal polishing will also change you outwardly: your facial features will become attractive, elegant, and intellectual. Men will become manlier and women will become beautiful. People will recognize you as a truly calm, noble person.

It may be helpful to think of meditating as being a bit like brushing your teeth—something that takes a little time each day. After several months have passed, big differences are sure to appear. If you believe this will happen, the results will be even more wonderful. Also, through Anugraha received privately, and through samadhi retreats, you can remove all suffering surprisingly quickly, and be beautifully reborn.

Life will become more abundant, and every moment will be enriched. Time spent working hard will be fulfilling; leisure time and even sleep will be just as fulfilling. Eating, not eating, even being out of work, having no money, or being ill—everything will be fulfilling.

Testimonial: Thinking Disappears, the Body Disappears, and Meditation Occurs

from a corporate employee in Tokyo

Before meeting Yogmata, I had done twelve years of meditation through a well-known organization. But idle thoughts continued to arise, and I had no real solid feeling in my meditation. When I picked up and read Yogmata's book, I intuitively felt that this was the real thing.

I started Yogmata's meditation and within a year my experiences of actual no-mind grew longer. I continued to enhance myself internally day by day and became able to safely and comfortably experience deep meditation. Then, when I received the secret method the other day, my body suddenly and truly disappeared, idle thoughts vanished, and I perceived with consciousness alone. It was amazing, and I felt as though I wanted to shout out with joy. I will never forget it.

Things are just as Yogmata said they would be. I am full of feelings of gratitude, happiness, and enjoyment, and I want to jump for joy because people can so easily experience the secret teachings of Himalayan Yoga. Words are not enough. Yogmata has my unlimited thanks and respect.

Doing Meditation Your Own Way Is Dangerous

If you go to the bookstore, you will see many books on meditation methods on the shelves. However, the authors have only recorded their own methods in these books, and the appropriate method can vary widely from person to person. If you meditate on your own using a method that doesn't suit you, it can be dangerous. What should you do to make sure you are using the most appropriate meditation method? The safest thing to do is to have a secret meditation method given to you through diksha from a master.

In India, there are many masters who give diksha, but the diksha given by holy Himalayan Siddha masters is special. A purification process called shaktipat—a special, secret ceremony not found in other styles—is performed. Following this, you are instructed in a holy wave meditation method that is for you alone. This purifies the mind, body, and soul with high-dimensional energy, and is something that awakens the energy centers within you.

These waves introduce you to deep meditation, quickly calm you, and will always protect you. Receiving a meditation method through diksha from a master will enable you to be reborn as an awakened person. If you truly believe, you will be protected for the duration of your lifetime.

It is important to trust yourself, to believe in the existence of higher dimensions, to receive power from them, and to proceed to purify your karma with constant peace of mind and gratitude. It is also important not to express discontent, worry, or suspicion, but to strengthen your gratitude for being given the opportunity to purify and transform. Believe in truth and trust in what you are doing. You will become your real self.

The Soul Will Fly Where You Want to Go

When we remove the body, the mind becomes free. If you have entered into deep meditation, and you think, "I want to fly over there," your soul will really fly over there. Or, if you inadvertently think, "I'm useless," you will fall into hell. If you have a grudge against someone, you will go into the world of grudges.

Haven't you had this type of experience in dreams? If you go to sleep thinking that your body is extremely heavy, you will likely have dreams in which you are crushed by a stone or fall to the bottom of a chasm. Therefore, it is important not to have negative thoughts when you meditate. Practice with belief. If the body shows symptoms, observe them. This is the process of purification, which removes distortion—symptoms will quickly disappear.

Also, during the day, when you're not meditating, foster the great energy of love and peace, with gratitude and respect, without behavior that creates needless confusion. Practice doing good karma for the sake of freeing the soul. Try not to injure yourself or others. In other words, continue doing good deeds with gratitude and respect, believing in yourself and believing in the invisible existence.

Even during meditation, if you don't have anything that connects to the deep truth of the source, you will be drawn toward the world of attachment and the workings of the mind. To avoid this, choose something that, for you, truly connects you to the deep truth of the source—God, Amida, Kannon, O-Jizo, the Buddha, a master—it doesn't matter. Amaterasu Omikami (the Sun Goddess) and the Great Bodhisattva Hachiman are also fine, as are Jesus Christ and Maria. But something that is truly connected to truth is indispensable.

Testimonial: One-and-a-Half Years Since Beginning Meditation, Everything has Changed

from a researcher in Tokyo

When I initially began meditation, I put all my effort into daily meditation and participation in seminars and felt that it had nothing to do with my job. But when I closed my eyes to meditate a little before explaining some documents in a meeting, I was able to calmly make my explanation without any difficulty.

I work in research (circuit design and development), so it's impossible to do anything without technical knowledge, and I don't have enough knowledge. But after meeting Yogmata and beginning to meditate, a year and a half ago, I am now able to speak in front of people with confidence. For me this is an amazing change, because I don't have much knowledge and was just floating along in the company, with no confidence whatsoever. Now I have become more confident, and I have been evaluated even though

I'm not doing anything big. My boss told me, "Your rating has improved," and I got a promotion. My head is clear, and I am able to work at a much faster rate than before.

Even though I don't have technical knowledge, I have come to think, "I don't know the details, but it's basically like this," or, "I should probably do this." I can't explain it well; it's not knowledge, but a feeling that comes from inside, a confident, full sense that "I understand." I think it would be amazing if I added knowledge to this.

I was lucky in this, too. The research I had done previously turned into an important project, and my evaluation rose again. More recently, I have been given important work that I can do, and which doesn't require much time. It's all thanks to Yogmata. I used to think of quitting the company; now I think there's no job as great as this.

I have truly experienced that "everything changes just by changing your awareness." I hope that as many people as possible will encounter this wonderful meditation and meet Yogmata.

Only Those Who Experience Samadhi Can Show the True Path

Meditation is the progress in this life of the process of purifying karma over many lifetimes. If you actively practice the secret method of examining yourself in just a fraction of each day, you will make this a reality. I would like you, every day, through meditation, to harmonize your mind and body, deeply rest, and come to be reborn. I would also like you to spend each day, in society and with your family, bringing others to life and giving them peace, while at the same time nurturing yourself.

The wisdom of the Himalayas is a strictly kept secret that can only be transmitted orally by a samadhi master. It is not simply knowledge, but an actual energy and a living wisdom. Once you begin to walk the essential path, you won't have time to be inattentive. You will become a complete human being and be given the role of bringing truth and happiness to the world.

It is good to detach from the surrounding hustle and bustle, to enter into deep stillness. But in order to accomplish this, a safe environment full of love, power, and wisdom is required. A true master guide is needed. You will become aware of your body, and purify it; aware of your mind, and purify it. By receiving the esoteric Himalayan wisdom, by receiving Anugraha, you will enter into deep meditation at once.

When this happens, your body will be still, your mind will be still, and everything will disappear. You will become no-mind. You are on the fastest path to samadhi.

10

⚬⚬⚬

Truths About the Spirit and the World After Death

The Words of Mediums and Channelers

Recently there has been an increase in the number of people who are interested in spiritual matters. Some people decide their day's actions based on divination, deciding to go in a certain direction or wear a certain color of clothing. There are also those who inquire of mediums and channelers (those who can communicate with the spirit world), and live their lives based on that guidance.

Some people ask mediums to look at their past lives and are happy to be told that they were a king, a princess, or a famous person in a past life. There is, however, no way to confirm whether this is true or not. It is good to take an interest in the past, but it is more important to live in the present.

There are many psychics in India, who enter a trance state, connect with people's souls, and see their past lives. This also connects to the level of the person's mind and becomes a receiving of their karma. This operation also strengthens the mind and is completely different from disconnecting the mind and freeing the soul, the path to enlightenment. Such psychics also have a strong mental energy. When these people say that your fate is such-and-such, or that a catastrophe awaits if you don't do such-and-such, there are only two ways to react: you can either submit and agree, or strongly react against. In either case, these words create attachment, a strengthening of the ego, turn into worries, and permeate the mind.

The important thing, always, is for us to know our true selves. We contain the past and the future, and we should be grateful for both the good things and the bad things in the past. From within our hearts, we must open up the things we have experienced, and release them. This occurs when you receive a blessing from a master.

By focusing the mind, undergoing meditation training, and walking the path to samadhi, all opens up, and your past lives appear clearly. Be aware of these things, transcend them, and return to the origin of the self. Free yourself from the workings of the mind of attachment. Control the self and become your master.

It's Dangerous if Your Mind Power Becomes Strong

Modern society is very competitive. Many people discipline their bodies and minds and focus their powers on accumulating information. They try to remain competitive by strengthening their minds and bodies. In order to create better things and live well, attain creativity, people become desperate just like fighting with their ego.

There has been a strong trend recently of attempting to strengthen mind power (willpower, the power of thought). However, such attempts at strengthening only lead to attachment, which then plays tricks on the person.

Of course, to master this and become successful creates happiness, but this joy only lasts for a brief time, before the mind starts busily searching for the next object of attachment, constantly changing, constantly battling—constantly flinging you around. This will never fulfil you within.

Even in the spiritual world, the focus is on constant training to strengthen the mind. In using the mind for healing and related techniques, it becomes changed and its operations are strengthened. Because psychics are constantly using mental images, visualization, and hypnosis, their spiritual abilities are increasingly strengthened. Most of the time, however, those whose work is telling people about their future and past lives are only speaking from their imagination. They have likely made great efforts to achieve the strength to control that power. But to use the mind in this way is not the path to truth. The mind tires and will never know real happiness. Imagination is always firmly within the realm of the mind, and in order to meet truth, you must eliminate the mind. Intuition and vision can certainly arise when the mind is emptied, but this is not what most psychics do.

If you become a person who sees past lives, you are proceeding in a completely different direction to the truth, the path of enlightenment, and the path of being liberated from earthly desires. The desire for mind power is usually for the sake of surviving in society by exhibiting various special abilities. But, if you strengthen your mind in this way, you will eventually grow tired and weary. Real happiness lies in stillness and tranquility.

Truth is released through becoming aware. This can then lead to the development of true abilities and success, to tranquility and enlightenment. If you have resolved to develop your mind power, you must also resolve to return to the original mind. You must purify the mind and release it, return to your true self, and be unselfish.

It's Essential to Purify the Mind Before Strengthening Mind Power

People with strong mind power can be magnetic and attract people to them. These other people recognize a strength they don't possess, and they aspire to it. But, again, real happiness lies in coming to have a mind of nonattachment and becoming a harmonious human being. When people become attached to special abilities they don't possess, the personal fascination can cause the mind to fixate, and the point of fixation becomes very strong. This results in distortion, which inevitably leads to suffering.

It's important for people with strong mind power to balance themselves and purify their minds. Usually, the purification of the mind is disregarded: people increase their abilities with the objective of attaining material things, bringing their desires into reality. The ego comes into play, resulting in extravagance and strong obsessions. Even in spiritual training, we find erroneous training methods that involve focusing without awareness, in order to gain power over others.

If such mind power becomes very strong, the ego becomes strong with it, and you must be careful, and take responsibility for your actions. It is all too easy for a strong mind to play tricks, both on yourself and others.

The Truth About Seeing Past Lives

While there are those who speak of the past lives of others, there are also those who want to see their own past lives. To truly see your own past lives means purification of the mind and release of attachment. Because of this, it is all but impossible to see the past lives of others.

A very few people do have the ability to lose the self and enter into a trance state, wherein they can see the past lives of others. Only one of a person's many past lives can be seen, at any given time. However, most people who claim to see past lives are speaking only from their imaginations (because people listen to and believe these words, healing does still occur).

There are many such types of mind power. The mind contains a record of the past and has the power to visualize images. Most channelers speak of past lives through images of the mind, but they also bring things from the past and the future, through hypnosis and the psychic mind.

The persuasive words that issue from mind power play tricks with people, and control them, for better or worse. This strengthens the mind that wants to open up such things. These words have a sort of temporary effect, which can, in some cases, result in healing. However, the behavior of psychics and channelers adds to accumulation of karma for both parties and leads farther and farther away from truth. It does not result in awareness, transformation, or release from within oneself.

If you want to create a good future for yourself, you need to do good things with awareness. Purify the mind, empty the mind, and return to the source so that karma doesn't play with you. Then, good things will naturally appear from within. You will have abundant affection for those around you, and you will become a great person with great personality without reason.

A Guide Is Needed for Progress on the Spiritual Path

Sometimes a person with a strongly repressed mind suddenly becomes a different person overnight. Such people have usually experienced some kind of discord and are suffering; they pray for peace and think that they can hear the voice of God. That is, they have had the power of their unconscious awareness activated and drawn out.

Dreamy young girls are often prone to such possession. People with little or no interest in the world of reality are also prone to embrace reverie, and people who like to indulge their own thoughts are prone to enter the world of spirits and become possessed. Trying to become someone special, they seek mystical and psychic power, or the thrill of looking at scary and unpleasant things simply for their own sake. If they are trifled with by impure spirits through dabbling in the spirit world, they could suffer greatly. If you wish to enter the spirit world, please be aware of the danger, and acknowledge the kind of karma you have.

The spiritual path can be extremely dangerous without the guidance of a master who knows it well. If you proceed on your own, the ego inflates, and the mind draws things toward itself. You have no way of knowing what will be attracted from previous lives. Your spirit? Someone else's? It is no easy task to control a strong mind.

The true path begins with trusting yourself. Purify your mind, purify your actions, become balanced. Understand everything with awareness. Leave the ego behind, aim for the truly high world, discard your strong, desiring mind, and become nothing.

This is the essential quest. From here, you will know what to ask for, and your aspirations will manifest.

Testimonial: I Became Able to Reject Bad Energy
from an office worker in Tokyo

In the seven months since I received diksha and the secret meditation method, many things have happened, and my mind has changed.

I accidentally dropped the bicycle on which I was carrying my daughter, and she hit her head hard, temporarily losing consciousness. It was very serious. Her left eyelid was paralyzed, she staggered when walking, fell down easily, and had headaches and nausea. However, there were no external marks at all—no bleeding or bumps.

I immediately began to offer up Yagya prayers. I began to think that this would also be something of a big karmic purification and calmed myself. Coming home from the hospital with my daughter, we were both tired and went to sleep. I think it was the next day at about four o'clock in the morning. When I put my hand on my sleeping daughter's head, it was red and very hot. I intuitively thought, "This is because I requested prayer from Yogmata; something is happening."

My daughter slept well, and I let her sleep until she woke up, at around 10:00 a.m. She was in good spirits and said with a smile, "It doesn't hurt anymore." Five months have passed since then, and her left eye is almost healed. I am happy and have given thanks many, many times.

I wasn't good with personal relations and disliked talking to people and getting up in front of people. So dealing with work, relatives, and school PTA meetings was agonizing—I would get palpitations and panic. When talking, I would falter. I felt as though I was paralyzed; I didn't have faith in myself—I only blamed myself.

What surprised me the most is that I became able to repel other people's negative energy. The need to bear grudges disappeared, and I became able to view my surroundings with a calm mind. I became able to trust myself.

My feeling of being protected by Yogmata is real. I clearly feel a difference when I have the protective charm given to me by Yogmata and when I don't have it. It repels bad energy and has a wonderful power. I also feel that the mantra I received suits me perfectly.

My daughter was born with two holes in her heart and was unable to move vigorously. When I received diksha, my daughter's edema ended and her urine volume increased, and when she received diksha (also from Yogmata) she became stable not only physically but also spiritually. She became obedient, happy, able to speak clearly and understand well. This meant that I, too, could work with peace of mind.

Around three months after my daughter received diksha, her regular medical examination showed that her heart enlargement had gone, and even the two holes in the damaged ventricle partitions had improved—the large hole had shrunk from 5.5 mm to 2.2 mm and the smaller hole had almost closed. The doctor told us, "The reverse blood flow has almost stopped, so she can live normally now. It's OK, because the holes are so small." I am full of amazement and gratitude for the power of Anugraha.

What Happens When People Die?

When people die, the spirit that separates from the physical body becomes the fine astral body. The physical body is burned, and attachments separate. However, samadhi Yogis and holy men have already purified their karma, so their physical bodies are not burned.

In Japan, those who treasure their ancestors hold memorial services when a family member dies in his or her memory and for the spirits of all ancestors. The deceased are enshrined and become the objects of prayer; if they died and went to heaven, they are prayed to for protection.

The spirit, as we know, is composed of the mind and the soul, and within the mind is etched the karma of memories and experiences. This includes the karma of the negative mind as well as memories of good karma, laden with good deeds. Spirits are reborn according to the fate of these various levels. However, not all spirits are reborn—those who experienced samadhi have purified and transcended karma, so they are not reborn. Also, those who die in accidents can't be reborn right away. This is because they died suddenly, not of their own will, and they still have karma remaining. In such cases, it is necessary for someone to pray for these spirits in order to help them.

People who go to hell because of bad karma may be reborn after a very long time. If they are able to eliminate their karma through extremely severe training in hell, they may be reborn. People who go to heaven because of good karma return to this world after many tens of thousands of years, after the benefit of the karma allowing them to be in heaven has been used up.

A Story of Rebirth

A holy man was told by his master, "Look after this person (also a holy man) who has died." The holy man continued in prayer, as instructed by his master. After ten or fifteen years, he contacted the dead man in prayer, saying, "Where are you? Have you already been reborn?" The person being prayed for had already been reborn and had become a holy man. He felt that he was being called and fell into a trance. His soul soon left his body and flew to where the praying holy man was. He said, "I've already been reborn, so please don't call me. I can't come here. Also, I don't know what kind of body I would return in, so please don't call me."

When spiritually powerful people call souls, such things can happen. If the called person's soul has already been reborn, it can create problems. Generally speaking, people pray to their ancestors to help them, but this can cause distress if the person has already been reborn (it can also become an obstacle to rebirth).

What Is Your Guardian Angel?

Even if family members don't pray, there are the spirits of ancestors that protect them. These are guardian spirits. The spirit of a good ancestor who did much good while alive becomes a guardian spirit that can help the family at times. It is an unseen existence that secretly lends aid.

Even if the living family doesn't make contact, the guardian spirit promotes success in business, guides people to good partners, and gives abundant harvests. Guardian spirits are not limited only to distant ancestors. When a family member with good karma dies, they can become a guardian spirit for the remaining family members.

The masters of Himalayan Yoga who are alive today can also be thought of, in broad terms, as guardian deities. Masters give diksha, make requests on behalf of a person's spiritual growth and happiness, and offer various forms of protection and guidance. However, because they live in physical bodies, they are not spirits.

By giving diksha, samadhi Yoga masters mediate between you and God, become one with God, and protect and guide you. They lead you to your true self, and to enlightenment. In the process, they transform your body and mind and make it possible for you to achieve happiness and success.

Through diksha and the blessing of Anugraha, you will awaken internally, while the purifying holy sound waves of your mantra protect you. Further, the holy waves that are created by yantra energy training and chakra training form a protective aura that surrounds you.

If you connect to God through a master, you will be protected even if you don't have the protection of ancestral spirits or the various gods. If something troubling happens to you, a message is conveyed to your master, who will protect you. You simply have to believe this, and it will happen.

When a master dies, they become a true guardian spirit. They have a responsibility to protect you because of the fate of the karma connected to diksha. You can, of course, also receive protection more simply, through prayer and devotion. High-level souls who have attained enlightenment don't need guardian spirits; they have the power to become their own guardian spirits.

The Holy Existence Called Angels

India is a country of faith. From gods such as Rama, Krishna, Shiva, Vishnu, Brahman, or Kali to masters such as Mahavir, the founder of Jainism, people choose their favorite Gods or a deceased master and pray to them for guidance. Buddhist believers believe in and pray to Buddha, Christian believers believe in and pray to Jesus or Mary. These become guardian spirits. The cedar-burning rite of Yagya can also function as a type of guardian spirit and provide a family with protection.

The Indian people also have living masters to whom they pray and from whom they receive guidance. However, since there are so few samadhi Yogis, there is practically no chance of having one as a master.

The teachings of Christianity contain references to beings called angels. Angels are nurselike beings that come from heaven to make children happy and protect them. They are holy male and female existences that have wings and can fly through the sky. Angels come to help when there is trouble or when danger is near. There are many angels, and they appear through your belief in them.

Auras Are the Light of Energy

There are entities called background spirits that are easily confused with guardian spirits. Spirit seers sometimes claim to see background spirits behind people, but this is usually simply a product of the seer's imagination. If there *is* something visible behind a person, it is their aura. Auras and background spirits are not the same.

Auras are the energy that everyone possesses, manifested as light around the body and head. This light is birthed by the energy centers called chakras. The color of a person's aura may change, depending on their state of mind, which is to say that a person's aura can indicate their state of mind.

Animals, vegetables, and fruit can all have auras. People who can see auras can sometimes also see auras around clothing when it has been taken off and hung up. While auras can't be seen by everyone, it is sometimes possible to develop the ability to see them by steadily gazing at someone's body directly after looking at the sun. There are five colors of auras that appear around people's bodies; these are the color of earth, water, fire, wind, and air.

In order to improve the color of your aura, you must train to purify your karma. If you purify your karma and chakras, your aura—the light from your chakras—can be improved. Shaktipat and Anugraha are very effective for this; they purify all of the nadis, including the chakras.

Cases of Spirit Possession

Background spirits are not auras. If a psychic sees a real spirit behind a person, it can be troublesome, perhaps even a serious obstacle to the person's life. If a background spirit takes possession of a person, that person's life is then controlled by the spirit—they no longer have a life of their own. Such cases are very rare, but they do exist.

In most cases, people who speak of background spirits have a mind that is fascinated by such spirits in relation to themselves—they are seeing something as a result of their thoughts. Psychics view others with a mind that has been developed through training to see such images. As a result, when mediums or healers say they have seen a background spirit, it is usually simply a reflection of their own minds.

We all have thoughts, attachments, and karma that exist as energy in our bodies and minds, and which we express in various ways. Through their imaginations, psychics tend to express this energy in the form of spirits. Then, they think this image, which they have created, is correct. People who consult psychics sometimes ask for such spirits to be removed, and there are certainly cases of people being successfully healed in this way. Enlightened people are able to directly heal people who have been possessed in this way.

When Channelers Contact Spirits

Channelers are said to have the ability to call spirits forth. They contact great holy spirits, gods, masters, and the spirits of dead people. Some channelers sit on chairs covered with cloth of a particular color, or sit in a special pose, and soon enter a trance state. Sitting beside a fire, their bodies sway to a background drumbeat, and they enter a trance in time with the rhythm and seek to contact spirits.

Such phenomena happen naturally to pure people who live in the forests and mountains, but channelers are different, wanting to do this whenever they wish. Most channelers are simply revealing illusions born of the movement of people's minds. Of course, there are some people who really do contact spirits, connecting to the past and contacting Einstein or Kennedy, or great spirits such as

Buddha or Christ, but this requires a great amount of training. This practice of contacting phantoms and spirits is known as occult or mysterious science.

Spirits don't have a normal existence, so it is not a simple matter to contact them. The possession of channelers by spirits involves the surrender of the self to that which is not the self, and the loss of that person's identity. Why is it necessary to become possessed by a spirit? We ourselves are powerful spirits. Also, among channelers are those who create images within themselves based on possession by the desired spirit. This is illusion, pure and simple.

If spirit possession was something that happened naturally, the person possessed would experience a significant unbalancing of their energy when they returned to themselves, as it is a very fatiguing process. Additionally, this becomes attachment to attaining a special ability, which quickly becomes extravagance. This is very different indeed from the science of enlightenment and the transcending of the mind in the service of truth.

Enlightened people, those who have attained samadhi, and samadhi Yogis are people of truth who have become one with God. These people heal through prayer of the holy will called sankalpa, through actual action—touch— and by simply being in proximity to a person. Such people of truth have no need to contact phantoms or spirits, neither of which are pure.

Testimonial: People Tell Me I've Become a Different Person

from an insurance salesman in Kanagawa

Until I met Yogmata, the inside of my head was always a jumble, and at one point I became depressed and lost interest in work and everything else. When I found out about Yogmata, I received diksha right away. Since then, I have received amazing benefits, even in areas that I am not yet fully aware of. My luck has improved, and I have met many wonderful people. I am full of ideas and inspiration.

Actually, the main reason why I started to meditate was that I didn't have a good relationship with my father, and I wanted to do something about it. Feelings of kindness, sympathy, and an understanding of my father's position began to sprout inside me, and although in the past he used to come down on me hard, he gradually began to acknowledge and accept me.

Although I had tried to quit smoking, I hadn't been able to completely quit, but after I started meditation, I was also able to do so naturally. Meditation gave me a peace of mind that I hadn't had before, and I also lost the need for sweets and alcohol. I feel that the good feeling I have in meditation continues to deepen.

Since I met Yogmata, people around me tell me that I have become another person—completely different from the negative person I was before. I have truly wonderful friends and I enjoy each day.

Don't Stop at Being Self-Satisfied with Volunteering

Volunteering is a service to people and to society; it is a wonderful activity and a beautiful way of living. But it can also be a problem, if you overdo it and damage your health.

While volunteering, in essence, is a beautiful reverberation, it can also cause you to become depressed, even as you are trying to help others. Rather than simply extending your hand to those in trouble, you could try to help them on their own journey toward peace and harmony, to become aware of themselves, and to be able to live with confidence. This makes things easier for all and enables true growth.

If, by extending your hand to others, those others become weak or arrogant, or if, through excessive volunteering, you fail to be sufficiently attentive to yourself, your actions become meaningless. Also, your good actions can have the opposite effect: you and the others can become unhealthily codependent, causing your mind to whirl in the duality between outward face and real intention.

If you are volunteering, you should always try to do so with a spiritual mind. Gaze deeply into your own mind and establish peace there. Then, you can volunteer with real love—a high-quality love, rather than dependent love. In other words, by spreading peace and love inside yourself, you become able to volunteer toward yourself—a volunteering of healing and transformation from a deep level, that affects other people around you.

Try to convey waves of wonderful love to those around you. Heal the people that surround you, just by being there.

By Turning Awareness Inward, Become a Person Who Doesn't Blame Others

If, in your daily life, you use feelings and thoughts that don't issue from your true self, desire and cloudiness will begin to spread in your mind. Gradually, you will only be able to believe what you see with your eyes, and even this vista will narrow, in line with your experiences. When this happens, misunderstanding and friction with others are the result, and your personal relationships start to spoil. If growth or development occur, they are only partial, and this creates imbalance, which weakens your life force and, if it continues unchecked, causes illness.

It is important to examine yourself, purify the mind and body, and return to the natural self. This is the path to becoming God, the path of enlightenment that leads through dhyana (stillness, deep meditation) to enlightenment. A life lived in pursuit of attachment to things, of stimulation of the senses and swelling of the ego, is not a life of true happiness. True happiness is attained by directing the consciousness inward and encountering the essence. Many people are becoming meditators, dropping selfishness, and becoming, one by one, people of awareness, people who don't blame others and who don't destroy nature.

We all have habits, and often we continue to hurt ourselves and others, even though we know this to be a bad thing. We make excuses out of self-defense and continue in our habitual ways. We may receive helpful warnings, perhaps from parents, or other forms of ethical guidance, but we conveniently ignore their real meaning and don't change our behavior. We say, "I understand, but I can't change."

To be conscious of the self is a start but, in order to become truly free from the mind, it is necessary to return to the source through receiving Anugraha to purify karma.

Ignorance Hurts People Unknowingly

It is as if some people have "Jinx" as a nickname. They don't intentionally do bad things, but they habitually express discontentment, think negatively of others, and grumble and complain. This transmits negative thought waves to others, and naturally jinxes the person.

Such people, without realizing it, create toxins within their own minds, resulting in a hateful energy that floats around them. Because of this, the person becomes depressing and annoying to others. If this is done in ignorance, it can be hurtful. By unconsciously judging and being mean to others, even though they are not directly doing anything bad, they are indirectly doing something not good; they are using an ignorant or desiring mind to becloud themselves and others.

What can be done to prevent this? You can know exactly who you really are. You can examine yourself. Reflect on yourself, be humble, rid yourself of obsession, and respect others. Try to develop the feeling that you truly want others to be happy. This is not just a matter of doing external things; you must harmonize yourself internally and become full of peace, live in good health, and not cause annoyance to others. This will contribute to the happiness of your family and the peace of those around you. As this circle expands, it begins to contribute to world peace.

Don't worry about the little things. Live with an abundant heart. Even if you become ill, try not to get depressed. Becoming sick is merely a readjustment in the balance of the microcosm that is inside you. And beyond that, it is an opportunity to examine yourself and face the truth.

There is nothing to fear. By having transformation into your true self as your highest goal, and by continuing to do good actions, you will free your mind and senses of bias, achieve balance, and live easily, with ample opportunity to exhibit your abilities.

11

Prayer Opens the Door to the Future: Seeking the Origin of Human Beings

Why Is There Divinity in Humans?

I have discussed the fact that our bodies are microcosms that have the same structure as the universe, that we are endowed with energy of the same nature, and that the great universe that gives birth to all is within us. Let's look more closely at what the source of human beings is, and what we can do to purify our minds and bodies.

We humans are beings created by God, which are reborn according to karma. At our source is an offshoot of God called the soul, which watches over us and aids our growth. We are born with a divine nature, and in this divinity are freedom, purity, and awakening. However, we have become disconnected from this fact—our minds have become too strong.

The mind is powerful; all behavior is brought forth from it. We are born into this world through sanskara, memory for the purpose of being born, and our minds are pure and unmoving; our divinity sleeps, and the mind hasn't begun to work. When we come into contact with society, the mind through experience develops: likes and dislikes manifest; and the senses develop. The mind becomes stronger through education, desires, ambitions, and karma, and our divine natures become further enveloped, and, finally, lost. Even the minds of babies develop quickly: their mothers embrace them, and the mind begins to work in response.

Adults tend not to think of the free minds of children. The opinions of society and the values of adults are forced on children; they are educated, our desires are projected onto them, and they are entrusted with our great hopes. Children are repressed and controlled by society, their environment, their families. They are brainwashed by the hopes and dreams of adults and lose their purity and freedom as a result. In this way, their divinity is gradually enveloped and obscured.

The Occasions That Awaken the Divinity Within Ourselves

When problems arise in life, when others treat us cruelly, when our pride is hurt, or when we become ill, it is an opportunity for us to ask if the path we walk is right or wrong. Do we suffer as a result of external phenomena, or because of karma? Who is at fault—us, others or society? Why do things always turn out this way? Is it fate? Destiny?

What are our true feelings? How do we feel, if we are honest with ourselves? If we start to ponder such questions, or pray to an existence that transcends ourselves, our divinity starts to awaken. We begin to realize that our various troubles have occurred through our experiences in—and the ideas of—society. Our behavior is being directed and controlled. Then we realize that we want to be free of such things, and free of karma. We become aware that there is something more, that we want to be returned to our essential selves. We begin to pray, and to visit temples and shrines:

"Please show me the right way."

"Please save me."

"Please give me strength."

This is how we pray to God or Buddha. Eventually, we meet with pure feeling and peace. Divinity has awoken within us. Even unhappy experiences and sad occasions become opportunities for divinity to awaken within us. A family member becomes ill, the family business goes bankrupt—these are opportunities for study.

Everything, in fact, can be study—training given to us for the sake of encountering truth. Use these occasions to deepen your awareness, control your mind, and become a person who is free. However, if your mind remains clouded, you may not be able to accept trying circumstances honestly. Feelings of resentment, anger, and defiance can be amplified, causing you to exercise poor judgment and proceed in a bad direction.

We are children of God. Although karma has built up and we have become disabled through the long process of rebirth, we have an original divinity, and our minds are blessed with an essential creativity. Our true selves are offshoots of God.

Know That All Things Are God's Creation

God lives inside of us: possessing a mind that is respectful of all things can increase our divinity. Plants, animals, all things—God dwells in them just as in us. Even though the level of divinity in humans, animals, and plants may differ, everything is God's creation, a part of God. All things exist for the sake of balance in nature.

When we know these things and a mind is born that honors all living things, a divinity that transcends ourselves naturally bubbles up from the egotistic way of life that is only concerned with protecting ourselves. On the other side of the mind that checks boxes, that ticks off likes and dislikes, is the mind of love, equality, creativity, and forgiveness. How wonderful it is to deepen your awareness, draw forth your divinity, and have it evolve!

Although we have the divine in our nature, we cannot control living and dying—these are God's areas. Samadhi is the only thing that transcends life and death. Samadhi is the journey to truth, and, in the ultimate samadhi, asanpragyata samadhi, or moksha, we become God itself.

The Relationship Between Modern Medicine and Spiritual Healing

Modern medicine has advanced at tremendous speed in recent times. Diagnostic techniques and treatments have seen rapid advances. Does this mean that spiritual healing no longer serves any purpose? No. Sometimes people who are seriously ill, or who have been in accidents, and don't know if they will live to see another day, can recover rapidly through the encouragement of family and friends. There are stories of those who were unconscious and who were called back to consciousness through the earnest entreaties of their family. This shows us that blessing and healing continue to be important.

Spiritual healing works slowly. This is because the process of getting well involves various stages. By passing through these, one recovers in a harmonious way. Blessing has a healing power that increases a person's life force— the blessing of a person of high awareness who is familiar with asceticism is particularly special. This blessing, as well as prayers of the will, called sankalpa, causes miracles of healing for those who have faith.

Sometimes, when a particular condition worsens as a result of spiritual healing or natural remedies, people complain or get angry. Please try to remember that spiritual healing works slowly. Often, for the sake of peace of mind, both for the ill person and their family, it is advisable to take them to the doctor.

It is important to have illness investigated by medical professionals, especially such serious illnesses as cancer. Spiritual methods that give hope can be a very helpful addition to conventional medicine. Believe that a miracle will happen. Such belief can result in great peace of mind and healing.

A Mind of Belief Brings Success and Health

Sometimes it is said that faith is evidence for weak people, but is this really the case? One cannot have success in life without belief, and belief in God is a significant part of this. Living without such belief causes the mind to become uneasy; unhealthy habits, loss of balance, or sickness are often the result.

We must protect our bodies from the attack of external stresses, escape our negative cycles, and cleanse our bodies and minds of toxins. Bad karma will cause you to be drawn to bad things. Cultivate awareness and try to correct bad habits. For example, cancer is usually caused by some form of disharmony or trauma. It is very important for people with cancer to have awareness. Change your frame of mind to one of gratitude and peace. Change your diet, if necessary, and exercise appropriately—such changes can do much to eliminate disharmony. Jogging, swimming, and bicycle riding are all excellent. Change your life, if you need to.

If you continue in ignorance, without changing your attitude, you are deceiving yourself and your condition will only worsen. If you feel where your illness is, you should go to the hospital and have it checked. Most of us accumulate toxins from mental and physical stresses as we get older, and our bodily functions tend to degenerate. The very latest medical technology is in no way at odds with spiritual healing. Why not benefit from the good points of both sides?

Healings Brought by the Body's Energy

Methods of healing differ, depending on the diagnosis and its particularities. But it is always important to purify the mind and body, maintain balance, and increase the life force. The life force becomes healing energy and can often heal the illness.

Yoga asanas (poses) are very effective for ordering and purifying the body. But it can also be very important to walk, jog, exercise, and relax. Of course it goes without saying that one needs to be careful not to overdo it. Practicing asanas, exercising appropriately, and relaxing gradually expels toxins that have built up in the body.

Food is also important for healing. Food creates flesh and blood, so it is always best to eat pure, fresh foods. Furthermore, choose a correct breathing method, and tune and purify the inside of your body. Tuning of the breath is done with the chest and abdomen.

There is a deep, secret teaching for healing, which involves awakening through purifying the throat nectar as the body's internal energy. Inside the head, deep in the forehead, is a center of undying energy from which drops flow; these are burned in the navel and used as life energy. Through the secret Himalayan technique of samadhi Yogi wisdom, these drops are controlled and received in the throat. By drinking this nectar, you can obtain unlimited life force and become immortal.

The navel is a center of life energy—solar energy—which is balanced, not too hot and not too cold. It can create a healing energy suited to the situation, which is then carried to the part to be healed. This healing energy is in every person and is sometimes referred to as the natural power of healing. However, it is very difficult to use such healing power on others. If used carelessly, your own energy can become disordered, your life force can weaken, and you can become sick yourself. Healing masters should have a profound knowledge of the mind and body and be able to control them. It is also useful to be able to increase your own life energy, if you want to become a true healer.

Expelling Toxins by Purifying the Five Senses

It is important to prevent ingestion of toxins from the outside, by purifying and controlling the senses. If one receives external stimulus, the senses go to work and the mind suffers. To prevent this, purify the senses and just observe sorrow and pain. Purification of the five senses enables you to control them, which leads to the purification and control of the mind. Kriya meditation, a secret Himalayan method, plays a big part in this purification process.

If you look at green, the eyes are purified; if you look at water, the eyes are purified. If you look at the sun, the eyes are purified. If you look at beautiful flowers, the eyes and mind are purified.

To purify the hearing, it is important not to get caught up in bad speech. Listen to beautiful music; listen to the sound inside your ears. Practice *kumbhaka* (cessation of the breath).

To purify the sense of smell, smell good smells. Practice breathing methods. Good air and good smells purify the body.

To purify the sense of taste, refrain from strong flavors. Eat natural, mild-flavored foods. Examine the sense of taste to avoid attachment to it.

Finally, purify the sense of touch—in other words, the skin. Avoid meeting too many people. Don't touch your skin. Bathe naturally, relax, and purify.

Control of the senses is the practice of the five steps of pratyahara yoga that was explained in Chapter Five. This includes a high-level practice in which you refrain from any action and examine what happens. Pratyahara contains many different components; you purify the mind while practicing concentration, breathing, awareness, perception, and control of the senses.

Please also be sure to move your body: walk frequently and awaken the body. Finally, breathe, sending prana—life energy—into the body to purify it. Increasing your energy is a guaranteed route to working well and experiencing success.

Yantras and Mantras that Purify the Mind and Heal Sickness

Yantras and mantras also purify the mind and have a healing effect. Yantras are used for healing by masters who know them well; they give the mind good thoughts and purify it. Yantras are not simple symbols; they express the great mechanism of the cosmos and the body. They affect your mind, body, soul, and environment, bestowing harmony and power. It can be useful to hang a symbolic yantra in your room. A master can ensure that you use the yantra that is right for you.

Mantras are holy waves that purify the mind—sounds created from the original sound of the birth of the universe, which become holy waves that are nurtured by masters who know truth. Through mantras, you can heal, and be invited to the source of life. Mantras are taught through diksha initiations given by masters and are a powerful life energy that is connected to the central energy known as kundalini. They have electric as well as magnetic energy. Mantra waves become lasers, which, when they hit the body's center, give birth to power. They can also heal at the cellular level.

There are three types of laser—or energy—that are created by mantras. These are (in Sanskrit): *sattva* (pure elements), *rajas* (active components), and *tamas* (heavy elements). Mantras cause transformation in you by purifying the mind, purifying the karma, and purifying the body. They have a chemical effect on your mental and physical systems, invite stillness and peace, and increase life force. Then, they awaken specific energies, heal you, and lead you to enlightenment. It goes without saying that it is very dangerous to practice a mantra without the guidance of a master.

Prayer Directed to the Heart

The heart is a center of love energy. By building up energy here, people develop minds of love. (This is not the love of attachment or possession.) Also, people become peaceful and happy. While this is good for you, it is also beneficial for others.

We are all siblings born of the same source existence. Our forms may differ, but our source is the same. Love the people around you, love the things you can't see, and be grateful. Pray the following in order to preserve peace and preserve happiness, for the sake of others:

> *May my body be peaceful.*
> *May my astral body be peaceful.*
> *May my mind be peaceful*
> *May all be peaceful.*

If the mind and mental state of an individual are peaceful, the world will eventually become peaceful. If you are peaceful, the way you should be, you can change your family, and you can change the world.

Prayer for the world is important because it becomes unified thought and mind. Of course, it is difficult to change the minds of many at once. However, prayer becomes hope, and, over a long time, it will succeed in bringing peace. By receiving diksha, receiving the holy waves, by aligning channels that transcend the individual, and by connecting at the level of collective consciousness, peace can be created.

But, in order for this to happen, the samadhi power of a master is needed. Through the holy waves of a master, various types of consciousness become one, and without it, the balance of energy is broken by human ego, and violence and war is the result. In order to prevent this kind of disaster, we must purify people's consciousnesses, and purify negative karma.

Let's spread the holy waves inside! Practice awareness and perception and pray for world peace. World peace is something God hopes for as well. Pray that the earth's environment improves, and that the world will one day know peace.

The Tremendous Power Called Prayer

Things—including you—are constantly changing. Creation and destruction are constantly repeating, at any given moment. If God decided to end the world, no power would be able to stop it. This would be a natural thing and is a possibility that always exists.

In our current era of difficulties, there are imaginative people doing spiritual work who fear for the imminent demise of humanity. This will only come to pass if God wills it (and if God wills it, it could happen at any time). Such is the power of nature.

Nevertheless, our prayers, also, contain tremendous power. Prayer affirms the mind and leads us in the right direction. People who pray connect to God and receive the power of holiness. If God wished it, people who pray would have no unhappiness in their lives. Prayer can change the mind, and it can change your life.

People who pray achieve the supreme existence called God. People who become their true selves are enlightened to universal truth. Through holy prayer, the door to the mysteries is opened. As humans, we are God's ultimate and final creation. God made us this way, so we can become God. Human beings who transform and awaken themselves are given the power to creatively change society and create peace in the world.

Through the Himalayan secret of Anugraha, you can make swift progress on the road to God, on the road to your true self. Then, when you receive the grace of God, your life will become abundant and happy. You will meet with success in every direction you turn, and you will be enlightened. Just as if you were looking inward, seated in a Himalayan cave, you will change with ease, and become your true self.

Afterword

In order to Purify the Mind, Body, and Soul

As I said frequently in this book, I am a yogi. I'm not a simple gymnastic yogi. I'm a yogi who knows the mind, body, and soul.

Because of my karma, I've been fortunate enough to meet the great Himalayan holy man who became my master, Hari Babaji, as well as Mahayogi Pilot Babaji, his senior student, and other great Himalayan holy men. I lived with them and had the opportunity to directly receive their blessing.

Through the grace of God known as Anugraha and the similar grace of the Himalayan holy men, I've been able to transcend the mind, transcend the body, attain Samadhi, and become self (the true self). I transcended time, transcended space, attained Samadhi, and became nothingness.

I then achieved the power to give blessing to others. I give them healing, take away their suffering, lead them to happy lives and give them success.

I know various techniques to accomplish this. I myself don't need to freely use those many techniques, only Anugraha itself is sufficient, but I convey those techniques in order to purify people.

Many people live using only the mind of ignorance and the mind of desire. Because of this, they make errors and experience much suffering and illness. I strongly desire that these be released and that people be guided to the source of light.

I convey to all people the things I learned in the Himalayas. Then I continue to help people who desire great growth in their lives to fulfill their dreams.

The Journey to the Inner World

In this book, beginning with examining the mind and clarifying worry and suffering, I explained the unlimited power, which lies in the world of nothingness, and why exactly people are born.

We aren't just born to eat, we aren't just born to work, and we aren't just born to have families and raise children. We aren't just born to enjoy life. Of course, we aren't born to quarrel and fight either. If we were born to gain the things we desire, to fight to live, and to fight to eat, we would be no different from animals.

No matter how much effort we put into work and even though we make frantic efforts to obtain that what we desire, when we remove the garment of our physical bodies and begin a journey into the other world, we must leave everything we own behind in this world.

I'd like people to be more self-aware of the way in which they should live, and the way in which they should die. It's then necessary to be aware of what is happening inside oneself and to be aware of whom exactly one is. I also want people to know what happens to our lives after we die.

When making the journey to the inner world, one understands with a true feeling what one's true self is. Inside you is the potential for wonderful abilities and power. You have unlimited potential. Inside you are true happiness and truth. You are a contented existence, full of love, a divine existence, a holy existence. I want you to be aware of these things.

All Things Are Wonderful Encounters

However, if such abilities and powers become caught up in a bad place, one will plunge into a hellish world such as that of Asura (a fighting demon). If one doesn't constantly raise the mind and lead it in the direction of virtuous energy, one will drop down into the depths of Hades.

I'd truly like you to receive these things sincerely, taking responsibility for the mind and body that you were fortunate enough to receive, and daily treasure and polish them.

Then, please let your mind become abundant, separate from thoughts and attachments, raising the level of your consciousness, and encounter the mysteries of the soul.

Please be led through nothingness to the world of the source, and achieve your dreams in this life. Then, please fulfill your role in purification of the world.

This is the study of all things while you're alive, an encounter for the sake of magnifying your love, an encounter that makes you aware of your wisdom.

> A Great Existence is constantly protecting you.
> Unlimited love transcending space and time is now being poured into you.
> You are full of peace inside.
> You are full of love.
> You are full of joy.
> You believe in yourself.
> The energy of the life force is activated within you.

I pray that you will become aware of deep, deep truth, acquire freedom, and walk a more wonderful, deeply abundant life that overflows with hope.

About the Author

Yogmata Keiko Aikawa was born in 1945 in Yamanashi Prefecture, west of Tokyo. She developed an early interest in yoga and naturopathy, which led her to travels in Tibet, China and India. She was one of earliest promoters of yoga in Japan, and in 1972 she founded the Aikawa General Health Institute, where she taught her unique Yoga Dance and Pranadi Yoga.

In 1984, she met the Siddha Master Pilot Baba while he was in Japan to perform a public Samadhi. He invited her to study among the Siddha Masters in the high Himalayas. There she met Hari Baba, who guided her through the final stages of Samadhi.

In 1991, Yogmata performed her first of many public Samadhis, a supreme yogic practice in which one is sealed in an air-tight, underground pit without food or water for seventy-two to ninety-six hours. After her eighteenth public Samadhi, she received the title of Mahamandaleshwar, or Supreme Master of the Universe, from Juna Akhara, the largest spiritual training association in India. Yogmata is the first woman and non-Indian to achieve this status.

She and Pilot Baba have held public teachings and initiations throughout the world as part of the World Peace Campaign. She is currently working with the United Nations on a series of international conferences to further universal peace, sustainable living and the leadership of women. Yogmata's charitable work includes the Yogmata Foundation, which is dedicated to funding mobile hospitals to remote villages in India. Her global mission is to bring love and kindness to all.

Today Yogmata lives in Japan. She has published over forty books.

Connect with Himalayan Wisdom

Email: usa@science.ne.jp
Twitter: @himalaya_siddha
Website: www.yogmata.com
Facebook: "yogmata"